Metamorphosis

JOHNNY MEETS JOHN

John Dewey Stahl

WESTBOW
PRESS

WestBow Press books may be ordered through booksellers or by contacting:

WestBow Press
A Division of Thomas Nelson
1663 Liberty Drive
Bloomington, IN 47403
www.westbowpress.com
1-(866) 928-1240

Because of the dynamic nature of the Internet, any Web addresses or links contained in this book may have changed since publication and may no longer be valid. The views expressed in this work are solely those of the author and do not necessarily reflect the views of the publisher, and the publisher hereby disclaims any responsibility for them.

ISBN: 978-1-4497-0109-3 (sc)
ISBN: 978-1-4497-0111-6 (hc)
ISBN: 978-1-4497-0110-9 (e)

Library of Congress Control Number: 2010925539

Printed in the United States of America

WestBow Press rev. date: 05/12/2010

To Audrey, Luc, and Ben:
John and Susan's grandchildren.
And to all growing persons, children and adults.

Contents

Pictures Credits

CHAPTER: BEGINNING PICTURE	SOURCE
1: My Family and Home	Family/John
2: Moving, Falling, Building	Sidney/ John
3: Cellar Goodies	John
4: To Cross or Not to Cross	Family/John
5: School Club and the Cache of Apples	Wm Joe Mabel/John
6: Things that Didn't Work	John
7: Ride through the Fence	Sidney/John
8: Visiting Preacher, Sharing and Prayer	Wm Lee– Commission Cents, Inc.
9: Doodle Bugs, Fireflies and Hornets Nest	John
10: Trousers and the Lamb	John
11: Snake in the School	Wm Furryscaly/ John
12: Passenger Pigeon/Morning Dove, Ivory Bill/Pileated Wood Pecker	Wm Key to North American Birds Wm Noel Lee
13: Blue Bombers and the Chinese Hat	John
14: Ghosts in the Chimney, Swoops in the Sky	Wm Chester A. Reed The Bird Book 1950/ Pearson Scott Foresman

Take a journey of the mind,
With a natural bent through time,
Not simply facts,
Not really fiction,
But experience remembered or imagined.

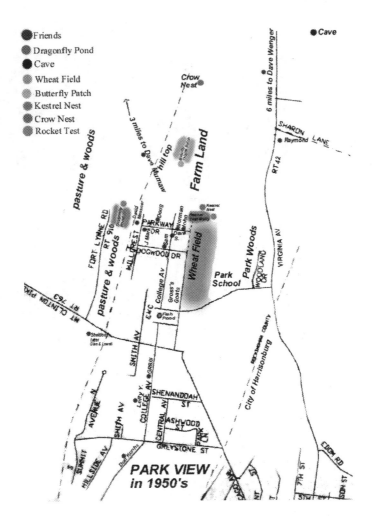

Friends
Dragonfly Pond
Cave
Wheat Field
Butterfly Patch
Kestrel Nest
Crow Nest
Rocket Test

Cave

6 miles to Dave Wenger

Crow Nest

Farm Land

SHARON LANE
Raymond

RT 42

3 miles to Dave Wenger

Pasture & woods

Museum hill top

Pasture & woods

FORT LYNNE RD
RT 910

MILL CREST

Parkway
DR

Dogwood DR

Kestrel Nest

Wheat Field

Park Woods

Park School

Park
School

WOODLAND DR

VIRGINIA AV

MT CLINTON PIKE
RT 763

College Av

Gross's Goats

Fish Pond

Sheldon Lane
Glen & Lois

SMITH AV

EMC

City of Harrisonburg

Rockingham county

AVENUE AL

SMITH AV

Leroy A.
COLLEGE AV

CENTRAL AV

GBBill

SHENANDOAH ST

ASHWOOD

PARK DR

GREYSTONE ST

SUMMIT

HILLSIDE AV

Don Kurtz

PARK VIEW
in 1950's

ELDON RD

7TH ST

8TH ST

SECTION 1: MOMMA'S BOY

CHAPTER 1: *My Family and Home*

I was the youngest in the family, but I hated it when Mother told visitors that I was the baby of the family. I didn't like being called "Johnny" either, but I got called that often in my early years. Our family was Poppa Dewey, Momma Mary, brother Omar, sister Anna, brother Milo, brother Jacob, sister Sara (four years older than me), and finally me, John, with Dewey attached in the middle. We were the eight Stahls; living first in Juniata County, Pennsylvania, in "Dutch" country. Our parents didn't actually speak Dutch, but rather Deutsch, a form of Low German. Poppa and Momma spoke only "Pennsylvania Dutch" until they learned English in grade school. They had only eighth grade educations, but both had done short Bible-terms of study in Johnstown, Pennsylvania and at Eastern Mennonite School, (EMS), in Virginia. As a small child, I learned to say and think that I was a "Juniata County Deitcha boo,"--a Juniata County German boy. However, only my oldest brother, Omar, could hold a conversation in our parents' native language. He learned it from our Grandmother.

While I was growing up our parents spoke only English at home, although it was, as some would say, "Dutchified." Jacob, Sara and I became so frustrated when we visited with relatives in Canada who spoke "Pennsylvania Dutch" that we started talking "Pig Latin" with each other. That's a made-up language we had mastered fairly well. "Anca ouya alkta Igpa Atinla?" means "Can you talk Pig Latin?" Can you figure out our code way of speaking this butchered English?

When I got to first grade I could not distinguish "v" sounds and "w" sounds. I said "wery" good instead of very good, which the teacher thought was very bad and I thought was "wery" difficult. It gave me a bad taste for language and English in particular when I had to stay in and practice speaking rather than going out for recess, which was about all that I liked about school at first.

I was a sickly little boy. The doctor said I had too much "nervous energy." Would that be called ADD or ADHD today? I was also dyslexic, and still am a little bit today. I get the letters, "g, d, b, even p" mixed up sometimes when I type or write. I was Momma's baby, and she had as much trouble letting me go to school as I was sickly. In any case, I had to repeat first grade. All these early educational woes didn't keep me from getting a Ph.D. later, and maybe even gave me an extra push in that direction.

Our family lived on a little farm in Juniata County, Pennsylvania that they had inherited from Momma's parents, Grandma and Grandpa Brubaker. I never knew my mother's parents because they died before I could remember anything. Momma was the baby of her family. So that made me the baby of the baby. Grandma and Grandpa Brubaker loved each other so much that they wanted to die at the same time, and their wish was fulfilled. One was unconscious when the other died, and the second soon followed.

We have no pictures of our Brubaker grandparents. Grandpa did not believe in "making graven images" as some of the strictest Mennonites called photos. Father's family, the Stahls, had no such restrictions about pictures. I can only remember Grandmother Stahl as a sickly old lady lying in bed. Grandpa Stahl had also died before my time, but there is a picture of him and Grandma Stahl. He was chief for a logging crew, made most of the meals at home, grew a good garden, and raised melons and cantaloupes in a field along the Susquehanna River to sell in the town of Selinsgrove, Pennsylvania. Poppa also remembered helping Grandpa Stahl dredge good hard coal from the river to burn in the wintertime.

Poppa was from Snyder County, Pennsylvania. That was a long 15_mile buggy ride from Momma's home in Juniata County. Poppa and Momma were cousins of sorts – Grandma Stahl was a Brubaker, like Momma.

The Brubakers were Swiss-German of Anabaptist-Mennonite stock. I am the 9th generation from Hanz Brubaker of Zurich, Switzerland. Hanz immigrated to Penn's Woods through the port at Philadelphia and claimed land along the Conestoga Creek in 1717.

The Stahl family made their way to the "promised land of the United States" some years later from Germany, and were originally German-Lutherans, but they may even have been Jewish some centuries earlier. One family story has it that a "many great" Grandfather Adam Stahl converted, as a long white-haired and bearded patriarch, to being a Mennonite. In any case, Poppa's family was Mennonite for several generations.

Poppa didn't join the Mennonite Church right away as a young man. He liked to play baseball for a town team, worked in the silk mill in Sunbury, and on the Pennsylvania Railroad with his older brother, Arthur, who was his buddy. Arthur was killed in a railroad accident in his early twenties. This was a life-wrenching and changing experience for Poppa. He made a Christian commitment, joined the family Mennonite church, soon put on a plain coat, studied Bible, and became a Sunday school superintendent. A "plain coat" was a special jacket that had no collar, and was usually gray or black. Adult members of the Mennonite church could immediately be recognized by this "plain coat."

Poppa had an unruly shock of blond hair and true blue eyes. Momma had straight black hair pulled back tightly under her covering and bonnet. The covering was made from a special pattern that identified Momma as a member of her Mennonite church. Her eyes were brown. She had been a good student in school. She was well respected, but she had turned down several prospective suitors. Her brothers became preachers, and I think she would have too if she had been a boy, but that was not permitted in the Mennonite church at that time. The Bishop of her church thought she was would make a fine wife for his son. The story goes that the Bishop, in announcing the "bans," the engagement announcement, of his son mistakenly said "Mary Brubaker" instead of the name of the bride-to-be, but then quickly corrected himself.

Momma waited until she was the then-unusually "ripe old age" of twenty-nine to marry Poppa, who was a year younger. By then Poppa had become a straight-laced Mennonite, but he also drove his own 1917 Model-T Ford, having bought the first car in his family. He still had a great sense of humor, and made Momma, who thought it important to be serious, "laugh too much" in their first year of marriage. On their honeymoon they visited Poppa's cousin who became the leading bishop in the "Black Bumper" Mennonite church. Too avoid being worldly, Black Bumper Mennonites went one step further than Henry Ford and painted their car bumpers black like the rest of the car, to avoid the appearance of being "flashy".

We six children arrived in this somewhat restricted world. Nevertheless, our parents wanted new possibilities for us. When the Great Depression happened, our family's fortunes fell. The Great Depression was a very bad time for the whole United States. Many people lost their jobs and their homes, and many banks and businesses folded. Father found some work in road construction, where he was paid 10 cents an hour. Mother scrambled to feed and clothe her growing brood of children.

One year our parents thought that there would be no gifts for us children at Christmas. Then our Uncle Harry came to the rescue with all kinds of wonderful gifts like dolls, dolly buggies, boys' toys and other goodies. The poor Stahl family had a wonderful Christmas after all! I don't remember any of this because I was born in 1939 after the Great Depression was lifting, and in the coming world war, World War II, the economy turned to boom times. My older siblings thought that I was spoiled.

Chapter 2: *Moving, Falling, Building*

*O*ur cousin, J. Lester Brubaker, from Lancaster, was attending high school at Eastern Mennonite in Harrisonburg, Virginia. He had encouraging words about this school for my oldest brother Omar, who was now ready for high school. Our parents wanted to get away from what they thought was the worldly dress, loose behavior, teaching of evolution, and support for the war of public school. Harrisonburg seemed like the "Promised Land" to them. Poppa, brother Omar and another educational immigrant, Hubert Pellman, took the family car, now a Model-A Ford, to spy out the land. The "ivy halls amidst the purple mountains of Virginia" beckoned hard. Our parents believed it was God's leading. The Stahl family farm in Pennsylvania was sold, and the family packed up in the Model-A to be off on an adventure to the new land of Virginia.

We arrived in Harrisonburg Virginia safe and sound, even though what is now a 4-hour trip took about a day's journey. We often had flat tires on such a long trip. No such bad luck this time. If it had happened, Poppa and the older boys would have had to unpack the car jack, lug wrench, air pump, and an inner tube patching kit. The bad tire would have been taken off, and its inner tube removed. Sometimes a nail made a hole in the tube. The offending spot would be sanded to make the patch stick better. Glue would have been applied to the spot on the tube, and then a patch applied and held tightly a few minutes. Then the tube was placed in the tire again, and the tire mounted on the hub, and the hub mounted on the wheelbase on the axle. The tube was pumped full of air again, and if the patch held we could be on our way. The whole process could take an hour or more.

We settled into a second-story apartment above a car repair garage that was a block away from the high school that Omar would attend. The other children attended Park School, a public elementary school, several blocks away. Poppa got a job working for a poultry hatchery. Everyone could walk; even Poppa could walk to work most of the time. A grocery store was nearby and a clothing store several doors away where "plain" Mennonite clothing could be bought. I stayed at home with Momma, since I was Momma's two-year-old little boy. The family was all settled in the "Promised Land" of Park View, a small town just outside of Harrisonburg's city limits. We felt that God had planted us here. Park View had a few hundred residents in addition to about 300 students who attended Eastern Mennonite School. The city of Harrisonburg had about ten thousand residents and less than a thousand students at James Madison Teachers' College and Normal School, a public Virginia college.

Like a normal two-year-old, I had learned to walk or run, and was running all around the apartment exploring new things. Momma was often working in the kitchen, and didn't always see what I was doing. One day I discovered a door that was usually closed, but had been left ajar, or maybe I discovered how to open it. It opened to a set of steep stairs that went down to the auto shop. I started down the stairs, but then I tripped and fell, and rolled the rest of the way down to the concrete floor. I was shaken up and crying. Momma heard the commotion and my crying loudly at the bottom. I don't know if there were men in the garage at the time who also heard me. Quickly, Momma ran down the steps, retrieved me, and comforted her crying baby. I was bruised, but had no broken bones. After that the door was locked, and I had no more misadventures down the stairs into the garage.

Poppa purchased some land to build a house in a new development north of Eastern Mennonite School. The development was being opened up by a man called Henry Brunk. Streets had been laid out and at first they were named after the Brunk boys, Henry, Perry, and Joseph (these names were later changed) but only a few of the streets and lots were ready to be used. The Brunk family had built, what to us Stahl children was a large mansion, on the top of the hill above the school. The property deed said that there were to be "no pigs" and that the land could not be sold to "colored folks." I don't think Poppa really agreed in his heart to either of these provisions. He raised hogs for a while until it was discovered and had to be discontinued. Poppa came from a church that had long had a black brother as a member, and he treated all black and white persons alike. Momma also came from a congregation that was the first to receive a black family into the Mennonite Church around the time that she was born, just before the beginning of the twentieth century.

The Henry Brunk land was good, and our parents bought it despite the stipulations. The nearest neighbors were located near the school, about two blocks away or on top of the hill, well above us.

The year was 1941, and we were still affected by the Great Depression, even though it had pretty well ended. We still didn't have money to build a new house, and it was difficult to get building materials because of the scarcity due to the war. Poppa found a large old house in Harrisonburg that was being torn down, just next to Blacks Run and across from what became the Water Street parking deck. He bought some of the old house lumber and hired a builder to construct a house for our family of eight as cheaply as possible. We moved into the first floor of the house even before the upstairs was finished.

I was too small to remember most of this. But I do have a mental picture of Poppa and my brothers driving up in an old truck with our household things. It was a good feeling. I lay down on a rug in the new living room with my baby bottle. The late afternoon sunshine was splashing a bright path across the floor. I was a contented toddler. Life was at peace, with a shining path to the future.

That was sixty-eight years ago from 2010, which now is that shining future. I don't live in the old house, but it stands proudly among newer ones just across from EMU, Eastern Mennonite University, the baseball diamond, track and soccer fields. The house has been beautifully restored, with the original oak floors, doors and window frames, and the oak steps and railings leading upstairs. It is still a white frame house, and stands in contrast to the newer architectures around it, with its large front porch, with round white pillars on red brick posts, supporting the porch roof. It is still a place to sit outside and watch the little world of Park View go by, but you no longer see Daniel Lehman making corn shock teepees, among which we children would play beckon or hide and seek in the field next to the Stahl house. The third and fourth generation of our Stahl family now lives in the house.

When I lived there, it was somewhat isolated from the rest of the community at first. We lived at the end of a long rocky lane that is now part of College Avenue. We walked to where we needed to go, and only drove to church and to go shopping in town. So little traffic went by that a Killdeer family built their nest in the middle of the rocky road! Only curious children seemed to disturb the nest. It was exciting to go near the nest. The parent sitting on the eggs would jump off the nest, acting like it had a broken wing and couldn't fly. It would flop around, crying in distress, and lead us away from the nest. After we were some distance from the nest, it would simply fly away no longer acting wounded. We loved playing the game with the bird, but we never touched the nest. We watched to see when the eggs had hatched. When they hatched, the little Killdeer were somewhat like baby chicks and could run all about. They don't stay with the nest, but learn to fend for themselves well before they can fly. Our little Killdeer were in no great danger of being run over by a car.

The Martin family had a farm at the south end of our Park View development. The farm supplied milk in glass bottles delivered to the far end of our lane. The rich cream was always the top layer of the milk. In summer the milk sometimes tasted like garlic if the cows had gotten into a patch of wild garlic. In winter the milk and cream froze. Then the cardboard bottle lids would pop up several inches above the mouth of the bottle. It was a nice cylinder of fresh frozen cream, and we children loved to eat it when we could.

Chapter 3: *Cellar Goodies*

*O*ur new house had a stairway going to second floor, and another going to the cellar. Most of the cellar floor was made of dirt, but on the west side, it had a high, wide concrete shelf. Soon I was running up and down steps and no longer falling. I had to expend the "nervous energy" that the doctor said that I had. The cellar was cool and a good place to play in on a hot summer day. Our cellar held many things. There was a bin that was filled with new potatoes from our large garden at the end of the summer. In that part of the cellar was also the place where Momma kept her wonderful molasses cookies. That should be a secret. You must pretend that I never told you about it. You should never, never get into the cookies.

Momma loved to work in the kitchen unless she was very sick. She knew how to bake bread and pies, cakes and cookies that simply made your mouth water. Sometimes we had "corn pone" which was a big pan of corn meal bread. It was very good and we made a whole supper out of it sometimes. But what I liked best for supper was that same pan full of short cake. Short cake was sweeter and smoother than corn pone, and didn't have a corn taste. With red, ripe strawberries and milk, it was a supper fit for royalty. Mother's lemon pies were not made with Jell-O lemon pudding the way some ladies made. It was a sugary, doughy lemon delight that baked to a crisp brown on top and tasted half like cake and half like pie. Momma was the best cook I knew. Well, I didn't like tomato soup so well, but then I didn't like most tomatoes, period.

However, on a hot summer day when we played beckon and sometimes got in the garden to hide, I, like the other children, might pop a little red cherry tomato into my mouth and it tasted alright. Now the doctor thought that tomatoes were good for me, at least that is what I was told. Maybe that was why I didn't like them. I thought they were medicine. So my family tried strategies to get me to eat them. You see, Momma canned lots of tomatoes in big quart jars. There were rows and rows of them on that large concrete shelf in the cellar. We had lots of canned tomatoes to eat, but I tried to avoid eating them.

Then George, who was about the same age as my brother Jake, got an idea of how to help me eat tomatoes. George and his parents had helped to pay to have the up-stairs of our house finished as a place for them to live while they were building their own house. George was like another big brother to me. His idea was to arrange all of those jars of canned tomatoes to look like a big air airplane. He knew I liked airplanes. I made folded paper planes to fly around the house or off the high back landing at the top of the steps the Brenneman family used to get to their apartment. I also had little molded plastic planes, and sometimes I bought magical flying balsa wood gliders at a little store in south Park View. Well, George got all those jars lined up to look like an airplane, but his prescription didn't work on me. I liked the airplane quite well, but it didn't make tomatoes taste any different to me. George later became a successful doctor to Native Americans in the West and later in Alaska. In fact, he became an expert on Native American diseases. He also taught as a professor at Johns Hopkins Medical College. I doubt that he ever prescribed a tomato airplane again.

Now when Momma baked molasses cookies, she baked lots and lots of them. I always wanted to help in the kitchen at that time. I could help a little by mixing the dough in a big bowl. The good part was when the bowl was empty. I got to lick it out, as we would say. It was a little messy because I ran my finger around the inside of the bowl to get out any leftover dough. Then I licked my finger off – yum, yummy! The cookies smelled good baking too. So I also hung around for the aroma. When they came out of the oven, Mother covered them with her top-secret glaze that made them shiny and smooth on top. Then she took an unusually large ceramic pot which she saved just for this purpose, and carefully placed the large molasses cookies to cover the bottom of the pot. The cookies were three or four inches in diameter. Once she had covered the bottom, she would tear a big piece of wax paper and place it over the first layer, followed by another layer of cookies, followed by wax paper, and repeat the whole process until the whole crock was filled with dozens of layers of big yummy molasses cookies. Poppa or one of my big brothers would carefully carry this whole big cookie jar down to the cellar, set it near the potato bin, and cover it well so that the cookies would last all winter. We didn't have a freezer in which to keep them, but this worked quite well if not too many people knew what was in that big crock. Shoo! Now I told you the secret a second time. Little children and even bigger ones shouldn't know where to find the cookies. Please, please don't ever ask me if I sneaked a cookie out of that big crock when no one was looking. I do believe, however, that the cookies disappeared a little faster than Mother served them to us or to our guests.

CHAPTER 4: *To Cross or Not to Cross*

*M*omma's good food (whatever I ate of it) was working and I was growing up. Soon I was ready to go to Park School with Sara and Jacob. There were two or more ways to walk to school. One way was to follow our long lane then turn left down Dogwood Street to what was part of the main road, now Park Road Drive. Then we would turn onto the macadam road, Park Wood Drive, which went by the school. We almost never went that way unless we caught a bicycle ride with Milo on his way to the high school. Milo would speed along on his bike and you had to sit on a little hard seat over the back fender and hold on tight. Usually it was a quick way to get to school. But one morning I was riding with Milo and he hit a big rock, which made the bike slide over onto the gravel. I got scratched up, but Milo's knee took the brunt of the fall. His pants were torn through. His knee was bleeding and even looked like it was cut to the bone. I was afraid, but Milo sent me on to school. He went to get Poppa to take him to the hospital. I didn't ride to school that way for a long time after that.

Usually I walked to school with Sister Sara. We would go down to the edge of our property to get to a farmer's rutted lane that went out to the main road. It was like walking a path through a little woods with trees and vines and bushes on either side. I often went there just to watch birds. Cardinals nested there. There were Blue Jays, Robins, Doves, Mockingbirds, Goldfinches, Wrens and sometimes the more elusive Yellow-breasted Chats. This was still a long way to school, but when we got to the main road we could walk with other friends and most of the Park View children went to school this way.

There was a shorter way to school that the Stahl children sometimes used. We lived right across a field from the school. When we were late for school, we would just cut across the field. It was a field in which the farmer had planted winter wheat. Winter wheat comes up like little blades of grass lying close to the ground to protect them from frost. In the spring it grows tall, and forms heads of wheat in the summer. The first summer we lived in our new home, the farmer's helpers came to harvest it. They had scythes with long curved blades that they swung to cut the wheat stalks. The cut stalks were then tied together in bundles. Several bundles were set upright and then covered with a bent bundle to form a little roof to deflect rain. These bundles were called shocks of wheat. They sat in the field until it was time to thresh the wheat, and made a pretty picture like little Indian teepees lined up in neat rows across the field.

Apparently we Stahl children were late for school pretty often, because the farmer told the teacher that we were making paths across his field and he didn't like it. We were told that we were not allowed to cut across the field anymore because we were harming the wheat. I was in first grade and not doing too well. I was unhappy and afraid of my teacher. She sometimes tapped naughty children on the head with her ruby ring. That really hurt even more than being rapped on the head with a yardstick. Of course our parents wanted us to obey the teachers, and a bad report from them resulted in a scolding at home. Once when Sara was in the classroom that I was in for first and second grade, the teacher stuck a sharp pencil in her head and made it bleed. Now you can understand why I was afraid and unhappy in school.

One cold morning I was walking to school with Sara and we were late. If we were to cut across the field we would probably make it before the tardy bell rang. Sara tugged on my hand, "John, we need to run across the field this morning." I was scared, but off we went as quickly as we could. That morning the teacher saw us or perhaps some tattletale reported us. We were caught. I had to face my teacher in fear and trembling. She said sternly, "John, you are never to cross the field again. Do you understand?" Of course I understood, but I was too afraid to say anything. Then she said, "Do you promise never to do this again?" I could feel Sara tugging on my arm in my head and knew that I would do whatever Sara suggested even if it was crossing the farmer's field. I was very afraid, but blurted out quite truthfully, "No." I just could not honestly say I would never cross the field again. That set the teacher off, and I received a good hard smack of her hand on my mouth. I cried hard, and can't really remember what happened after that. I knew that I would have to try hard not to cross the field. I don't really know how Sara's teacher dealt with her, and I probably didn't want to know. For a long time we walked around the field. But then there came again a time when we were really late. We heard the last bell ring and everyone went into the school. No one was watching. Sara tugged on my arm, "John, I am going to sneak across the field." I really felt small and afraid, but I followed Sara. We were late and got rebuked for that, but the teachers never found out what we had done that morning. I guess I did tell the teacher the truth.

Later that year, I got sick and didn't go back to school for the rest of the year. Mother seemed glad to keep me at home. I was often kept in bed, but didn't always understand why. A nurse came and gave me shots on my small bottom. I got so many shots that both little bottom cheeks were sore. When I finally got out of bed for good, except to sleep at night, I was ready to return to school. Our family attended that first grade teacher's wedding in the Brethren Church, which is now Community Mennonite Church in Harrisonburg. She married a preacher. The really good part was that she was never my teacher again.

I sometimes did get light taps on the head with a yardstick when I didn't pay attention in reading class. That got my attention, but didn't really hurt. I wasn't so excited about reading "See Dick run, see Jane walk, see Spot jump," umpteen times. I was never as frightened of a teacher again, and somehow I learned to read, but probably with a "Dutchified" accent. However, reading soon became an escape from things that I didn't like, and I became a real bookworm. I particularly liked horse stories and dog stories. Animals were my best friends. I dreamed of owning a pony like Virginia Ann Shenk, the daughter of my father's boss, Jacob Shenk. We were too poor for that, and had no place to keep a pony, but we did have dogs and cats.

CHAPTER 5: *School Club/Cache of Apples*

The school grounds used to be the county fair grounds. Behind the school was a line of large oak trees that provided an abundance of acorns for throwing and for frisky squirrels. Supposedly these trees had been the center of a horse race track. Our play area was quite level since it had been a racetrack. To the west was a high bank or wall against the farmer's wheat field. Wild strawberries grew there in abundance. They were tasty treats in late spring before school was out. At the far north end of the playground were old boards and some building blocks in a messy heap. I don't know how they got there.

I had been reading stories about the "Sugar Creek Gang." It was a boys club, not a crime gang like we know today. I thought it would be a good idea to start my own club, and thought we could build a clubhouse with boards and blocks. David, my good school friend who lived in the country, liked the idea. His Mother called us David and Jonathan because we spent a lot of time outdoors together. One of the smaller boys, whom I defended from bigger bullies, also joined the club, and several other friends like Lefty and Don. We gathered the blocks and started building walls. It took up a lot of recess time. When the walls were finished we laid boards across them to form a roof. We heaped piles of oak leaves on the boards to make it more rain and lightproof. We also piled leaves on the inside to make the ground soft for sitting on for our little "Pow wows." We thought we were true Indians. I even made membership badges out of small pieces of copper pipe that I had flattened and on which I had scratched our names. We felt like a true club, for we had all worked hard together.

There was one bigger boy in our school. We couldn't understand him very well. He was different, and we didn't seem to know how to become friends. He used to stand up and stick out his belly and say, "I am a Dutchman big and stout, with my stomach sticking out, because I eat mashed potatoes and sauerkraut." He didn't like that we had a clubhouse. He tore it down and told the teacher that we had destroyed his clubhouse. The teacher must have understood what really happened, and the boy didn't disturb us again. We rebuilt and maybe even improved our house.

In the fall someone brought baskets of Golden Delicious apples to the school for all the children. It was supposed to keep us healthy. There were lots of them. The club pooled our share of apples, and made a nest of leaves in the clubhouse for the ones we wanted to save. We covered them well with other leaves so that they were hidden and wouldn't freeze. We had apples to eat most of the winter. Our club had a great time together, planning many activities, but it was mostly David and I who carried out our ideas.

CHAPTER 6: *Things that Didn't Work*

I still hit some bad bumps along the way. I didn't always think very straight, and to be honest that still can be a problem even for a grandpa! Sheldon was one of my early school friends. Our fathers both worked at the Shenk Hatchery, the biggest poultry hatchery east of the Mississippi River. After several years, Sheldon's family moved to a home in another school district so I didn't see him again until high school. But in this story, he lived on Mount Clinton Pike just over the top of our hill to the west. The house he lived in had been a large plantation house. Before the Civil War, it was known as the Shands Plantation, and the white people who owned the plantation had slaves. In recent years the plantation house has been turned into a halfway house for released prisoners known as Gemeinschaft.

Sheldon walked home from school just like me. Sometimes we walked part of the way together, but I soon had to turn north to the Stahl homestead, while Sheldon continued on to the west. One afternoon we were walking along together and Sheldon suggested that I come along home with him to play awhile. I didn't think of asking anyone if this was alright, and I would have had to walk all the way home to do so. We didn't have the slightest clue about cell phones in those days. I just kept walking with Sheldon until we came to his house. It was a big place to explore, and we found lots of interesting things to do. Sheldon was called in to supper before I left for home.

I got home after six o'clock. Mother was all upset and worried about me, and Poppa was already home from work. "Where in the world have you been all this time, Johnny?" Mother scolded. "Just to Sheldon's house to play," I answered. "You should have asked first!" Mother scolded again. "I was worried sick. No one knew what had happened to you." I could see that Father was feeling very unhappy too. Mother said to Father, "Poppa, you need to spank this boy. The rod of correction will drive foolishness away."

I could see the look of dread on Poppa's face. He had never spanked me, nor had Momma. She wouldn't have wanted to herself and she believed it was a father's duty to mete out this kind of correction. I didn't know what was going to happen. I did know that Mother ruled the roost when she was in that frame of mind. In the corner of the room was a bow stick that I had made to shoot arrows. Poppa saw it, and slowly reached his hand to pick it up. Then he picked me up and bent me over his knee. He gave me several hard raps with the stick. I began to cry. I could see that Poppa's face was white. I knew that this was hurting him as much as it hurt me. Mother was no longer angry and scolding, but I went to bed without my supper. Well, I guess I learned a lesson. I never went to a friend's house without asking again.

Poppa was really my friend in many ways. He made jacks for us to play with since we didn't spend money on such things. He cut a part of an old broomstick in quarters length-wise, and then hollowed out spaces for the jack arms. He tied the stick together again, but had a hole in the upper end. Then he melted lead in a steel can, and poured it into the hole in the top of the stick. He had probably learned this skill from his own father, Grandpa Stahl, whom I never knew except from Poppa's stories. Poppa made enough jacks so that we could play the game with a little rubber ball. Sara and I and others played jacks together. You dropped the ball and grabbed a jack and then tried to catch the ball again. If you missed, it was the other player's turn. When the jacks were all picked up, the player with the most jacks won. Older siblings played it too. We liked Poppa's game.

Some Sunday mornings early before going to church, I went with Poppa to Shenk's Hatchery. It was his job to feed and water the baby chicks. The chicken pens had long feeders just outside their cages that they could stick their heads into to eat. Poppa made sure each feeder had plenty of food. I would go along after him and use my hand to push the feed close to the cage where even the little chicks could peck at it. Then we would come home and get ready to drive to church.

My older brothers raised rabbits in a rabbit hutch outside the coal shed near the big chicken house. They would kill and dress the rabbits. Dressing means that they pulled off the skin and fur and took out the intestines. They would then peddle the meat around Park View for extra pocket money. The rabbit hutch now stood empty. I had been reading about homing pigeons, and badly wanted to have some of my own. I begged Poppa to let me have pigeons and keep them in the old rabbit pen. He finally agreed, but told me I would have to earn the money to buy them and to pay for their feed by doing extra chores.

The day came when I had enough money to mail order several pigeons, and buy feed and special minerals that they needed in small quantities to keep them healthy. I fixed up the old pen, and formed a little wire gate that the pigeons could push to get into the pen, but inside pigeons could not open to get out. Finally my pigeons arrived and I did the regular chore of feeding and watering them every morning and evening. I knew how to do these things because

I watched and helped to care for our two flocks of chickens in the big and little chicken houses on both sides of the pigeons.

After they were settled into their new home, I carried one out into the field next to us and released it. It did return home and went back into the pigeon house or "dove cote" as we called it. I even bought some fancy pigeons and doves. The fantails strutted around with their tails raised and spread like tom turkeys, and tumblers did flips when they flew. The homing pigeons knew how to fly away and return without difficulty. But once I persuaded Poppa to drive me and one of my pigeons to the town of Broadway, about twelve miles to the north. I released the pigeon, but it never came back. However, a strange homer joined my little flock and made up for the loss.

Things were going pretty well, but in the winter the water froze in the watering dish and I had to break out the ice and give the pigeons fresh water every morning. By now, I was learning some basic chemistry and physics and I knew that salt keeps water from freezing if it didn't get too terribly cold. I got the bright idea to put some of the salt minerals that I kept in a separate dish for the pigeons to peck at whenever they felt the need, into the water. The next morning the water hadn't frozen. It seemed to work, and I thought I was a bright boy. A few days later, several of my pigeons died. They didn't seem to want to drink their salty water. I had a disaster on my hands! I went back to the former watering plan, and no more pigeons died. I think Poppa knew what was happening, but he never scolded me. I had learned another lesson, but this time I didn't need to be spanked to learn it.

CHAPTER 7: *Ride through the Fence*

*L*indale Mennonite Church was our home church. It was a five to ten minute drive north on Route 42. My friend David lived on a farm just next to the church. Linville Creek ran through the farm. Sometimes I went fishing there with David and other friends. Sometimes we could even swim in the creek. I liked going there, but I also liked to go to Morning View where my parents helped with the small mountain church. The church had benches made of two boards, one for the seat and one for the back. They weren't good benches to sleep on, or even to sit on for long periods of time. In winter, a small pot-bellied stove heated the church. You roasted on the side of the church near the stove and were cold on the side away from the stove. In summer, insects flew in the open windows. If there was a meeting at night, the lights attracted big beautiful moths from the woods around the church.

It was a twenty or thirty minute drive in our old Model-A Ford to another Mennonite church, Morning View, on a mountain ridge west of the quaint little town of Singers Glen where the early American songbook with soprano, alto, tenor and bass parts was published by Joseph Funk. Mennonites loved their four-part singing, but it wasn't done as well at Morning View as it was at Lindale. In either case, I really didn't do too well at singing parts. I once overheard Poppa say to Momma, "John can't keep a tune."

Poppa usually drove the car, but oldest brother Omar was also a driver by now. I sometimes got to steer the car on backcountry roads while sitting between Poppa's legs so I could reach the steering wheel. But I never got to do this on the way to or from church.

Omar was grown now, and seemed to have many grown-up things to attend to that a little boy like me didn't understand. One morning after church, we all packed into the car. Omar was the driver. I was sitting on the front seat between Omar and Mother. We didn't have seatbelts in those days and certainly not child seats. Riding between Mother and Father in a Shenk truck, used to deliver chicks, I once got a good bump on the nose and head when Father had to stop quickly. I still rode in a similar position in the car quite often, and no one had second thoughts about it being dangerous. That Sunday Father was sitting in the back seat with Anna and Jake and Milo. For some reason Omar was in a hurry, and was driving much faster than Father usually did. We leaned one way and then the other as Omar cruised around curves on the hilly road. As we topped one of the hills, Mother finally called out excitedly, "Omar! You're driving too fast." But it was already too late. Omar couldn't make the curve that he hadn't seen until he got over the hill. There was a fence straight ahead. The car smashed right through the fence into the pasture. Luckily, we didn't hit a fence post or big rock. The car swayed dangerously, but it didn't roll over. Finally we came to a stop in the middle of the field.

We were all shaken up, but no one was seriously hurt. Poppa crawled out of the back and took over the wheel. Omar slunk sheepishly into the back seat and didn't say anything the rest of the way home. That was something, because Omar was the big talker in the family. Poppa restarted the car and put it in gear. It crept forward a little wobbly. There was a farm gate ahead. One of us got out of the car and opened it. Poppa drove through onto the farm lane and then he stopped. He got out and examined the damage the car had done to the fence. Then he turned back and walked over to the farmhouse. A man had come out of the house and was standing there and watching after all the racket we had made. Father talked with him. It turned out that this man had helped to lay the bricks for the chimney of our house. Father apologized to him and promised that he would be back the next day to fix the fence. Fortunately, there were no farm animals in the pasture so the man said it was okay to wait to fix the fence.

Father drove slowly the rest of the way home. The car still wobbled. The front axle had been bent. I don't know what it cost to fix everything. I suppose brother Omar had to pay or help pay for the repairs. I'm sure it took a lot of Father's time to see that everything was repaired correctly. The car drove quite well for a few more years. I don't think that Omar drove that fast again. His important business could wait until we got home safely.

CHAPTER 8: *Revival, Sharing and Prayer*

I don't know if it was Momma's reputation for good cooking or the fact that we had more space after the Brenneman family moved into their new home, but we often hosted visiting ministers. I was usually too shy to say much more than hello to a preacher, and maybe not even that if I could help it. I can even remember hiding behind a door when cousins from Pennsylvania came to visit when I was smaller. But now I was nine years old, and I knew that such behavior was not acceptable. That year, Roy Koch from Canada came to hold evening revival meetings at Lindale Mennonite Church. He stayed at our place. He talked to all of us children and made us feel important. He even gave me a big copper Canadian penny, almost the size of an American quarter. It had a picture of King of England on it. It was the oldest penny I had ever seen. I treasured it for many years.

Of course, our family attended the revival meetings every night. I listened closely to what Roy preached. I had a disturbing feeling in my heart about bad things I knew I had done. Some of my friends and schoolmates like David and his sister Mary Beth raised their hands or stood up showing that they wanted to accept Jesus as their savior. My sister Sara and my classmate Mary Ellen were also in this group. I sat frozen in the pew night after night, with my heart pounding in my chest when the invitation was given, but I just could not raise my hand or stand up. I was afraid to speak with the preacher or my pastors about my condition. I was too shy, and didn't even want to be noticed. So I sat through the whole revival week and didn't make a public decision. I did know in my heart that I wanted to be a Christian. Roy went home to Canada, but I carefully kept my new treasure, the big Canadian penny.

Our Mennonite Bishop, J. L. Stauffer, started church instruction classes in preparation for baptism of those who had made public decisions. In our church, baptism was something that we had to decide to do, after we decided to be Christians. Our church did not baptize babies, the way some other churches did. I was deathly afraid of our bishop, but I respected Brother Stauffer, as my parents called him. To me he was a very imposing man in his black plain Mennonite coat. He was also the President of Eastern Mennonite School. But what stuck in my mind the most was a story Poppa told about Brother Stauffer. Before he became a Christian, he had wanted to be one of Pinkerton's men. This was a sharp shooting law enforcement group in Chicago, I believe. J. L. Stauffer was a deadeye shot, Father said. In those days most families had garbage heaps somewhere, mostly out of sight. They attracted some birds, but mostly rats. Father said that someone had seen Brother Stauffer step out his back door with a rifle. He looked at the rats in the garbage, and picked them off with his rifle shots faster than they could run away. I held Bishop Stauffer in awe.

My conscience kept bothering me about making a decision for Christ. I finally told Mother that I wanted to become a Christian. She was very happy and said that she would tell Brother Stauffer. The instruction class was to be at our house in a few days. When the time came for the class, I ran upstairs to hide. Mother came and found me, and persuaded, maybe almost forced, me to come downstairs. In fear and trembling I came down to talk to Brother Stauffer. He asked me some questions. My answers must have been satisfactory enough, because he prayed with me, and told me that I could join the instruction class.

I participated with the other children in the class discussion and answers. We had several more classes at other children's houses. After the last class, Brother Stauffer told me that I had a very good understanding of the plan of salvation for a boy as young as I was.

Brother Stauffer explained exactly how baptism would take place. First he would ask each of us questions about our faith and our desire to be baptized and give and receive counsel in the congregation. The answers would be "yes" or "I do". Then Brother Stauffer would cup his hands over our bowed heads as we were kneeling. Pastor J.R Mumaw would then pour water into Brother Stauffer's hands and he would let it flow down over our heads, after which he would shake our hands and help us to stand up while he said that we should arise to newness of life. Then he would give each boy a holy kiss on the cheek. His wife would kiss the girls. He warned us that the water would seem funny and might even tickle us, but that it was a solemn occasion and we should not laugh. A towel would be used to dry off the excess water. Then others would greet us as fellow members in the church.

On the day of our baptism I was almost sick with fright. Somehow I managed to take my place with the other children to be baptized at the front of the church. I would have been glad to drop through the floor with all those persons in the congregation looking at us. It went pretty well until Mary Ellen was baptized. She may have been as nervous as I was. When the water ran down her neck and back she let out a nervous giggle. I couldn't help but blurt out laughing too, and some other children did as well. I don't think Sister Sara did though, but she was four years older than most of us. I can't remember the rest of the service, but I believe that my face was as red as a beet for a while. I know that I was embarrassed and blushing. Somehow it all worked out, and I got home to be alone with my family, but I was a new Christian and Mennonite church member.

I wanted it to make a difference in my life. When the pie was cut and passed at the table, I didn't butt in for the first piece. I believe that Sara got it that time. I tried to listen better to my parents and to really be obedient. Brother Omar sent me an encouraging letter from Knoxville, Tennessee where he was teaching in a Christian grade school and studying at the nearby university. It was probably the first letter I ever received. It was written in Omar's flowing, fancy handwriting that seemed almost perfect to me. I thought that he had the best handwriting of anyone in the world except maybe his penmanship teacher, J. R. Mumaw. My writing was a scrawl and crooked. That was the way we thought all doctors wrote, but I had no plans to be a doctor. Omar's letter was dated October 25, 1948. He wrote, "Dear John. As I sit in my easy chair with my feet sticking under the covers of my bed, my mind is thinking of you tonight. ... My heart was made very happy when I heard that you let Jesus come into your heart. To live for him, John, will make you happier than all the money of all the millionaires in the world put together." After three pages of admonition, and telling me about teaching at the grade school, he closed as follows: "God has a perfect unmarred plan for your life. It is as lovely as the most wonderful snowflake that ever touched the earth. ... Jesus loves, and keeps, and satisfies. Walk arm in arm with Jesus. Your brother, Omar." That letter had a three-cent stamp on it, so you know it was a long time ago!

The following summer was my 10th birthday, and the family was having a party for me. I know it was fun, but this is what I remember the best. I had been praying for a baseball glove for a long time. I'm sure my family knew what I was hoping for the most. At the party, in addition to my favorite cake, and the smaller gifts from my friends, there was a nice big box. When I opened it I found the glove of my dreams and of my fervent prayers. I was a happy boy. It was a great 10th birthday.

CHAPTER 9: *Doodle Bugs, Fire Flies, and Hornet's Nests*

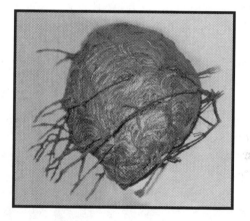

*O*n a warm summer evening, we children were sometimes permitted to play outside after dark. As it got dark we would soon stop playing tag, Anthony over or kick the can because we couldn't see well. Neighbor children would often be called home. But then a new magical world began. Little blinking spots of light would begin to rise up from the grass and the bushes around our yard. We called them "lightning bugs" or "fireflies." They are not bugs or flies at all, but they do fly. They really are a kind of beetle. They have wing covers like all beetles do that close over their true wings when they are not flying. Their two wing covers meet in the middle of their back and form a straight line. Bug wings overlap when they fold up, and flies do not have wing covers at all.

We would catch the fireflies in our hands. We could see that the bottom part of their bodies was where the flashing light occurred. To say it more scientifically, the last several abdominal segments were the flashing lights. Sometimes we would even squash the poor little beetles' back ends and smear them on our hands or foreheads. The lights would no longer flash, but did give a steady glow until they faded. We could see these spots on each other as we ran around the lawn in the dark. We didn't have lamplights on our street, so it was really dark unless the moon was shining.

What we liked doing best was to run into the house and get a pint sized glass jar with a metal lid. We would then take a nail and hammer and punch holes in the lid so that air could get into the jar. Then we would see who could catch the most fireflies to put into our jars. The jars would be our magic lanterns. If we had dozens of the little beetles in our jar, it made a nice magical blinking lantern.

After church services at Morning View, we would play in the woods while the adults talked. There were all kinds of interesting things in the woods. Sometimes when we turned over a rock we found little black salamanders that looked like little wet lizards. Sometimes we found little conical craters in the sandy soil that looked like the inside of a funnel made of sand. If you poked into them with a small stick, the sand at the bottom of the funnel would begin to erupt like a little volcano. Soon you would see a big crab-like pincer that was throwing sand. Then the head with the pincers might appear and finally the body of a little brown insect. These were "doodlebugs" that were larvae of an insect called the "ant lion." When an ant wandered into the doodlebug trap it would slip on the sandy slope of the cone-shaped crater. The doodlebug at the bottom would throw sand at the ant and make it slide deeper into its hole until it could catch the ant in its pincer and eat it. We would catch an ant and drop it in the hole just to watch what happened.

Sometimes driving to or from church we would see what looked like a gray bag six to ten inches in diameter caught in the limbs of a tree or a bush. Once brother Omar stopped on a winter day and got one that was extra large. It felt like it was made of paper. It had holes so that insects could crawl in and out of their paper house. This was a hornets' nest. Hornets are bigger than honeybees. Their stings are very painful and they can sting many times. Fortunately, since it was cold, no hornets came out of the nest. Omar took it upstairs and put it in the big boys' bedroom. After a day or so the hornets warmed up and started coming out of their nest and flying around the bedroom. Now it was a dangerous place. Someone was finally brave enough to get the hornets' nest and take it out side. After most of the hornets were gone, we brought it into the house again. If you come to our house, you might just see a big hornets' nest that we keep in our house as decoration.

Stahl Family and home in Virginia

Momma 13

Momma and Poppa in their youth.

Poppa as Boy

SECTION 2: GROWING BOY

Chapter 10: *Trousers and the Lamb*

$\mathcal{W}$e had several dogs after our first dog, Frisky. These dogs were smaller, and I was bigger now, so I liked to play with them. The one I liked best we called "Trousers." I surely don't know how he got that name. He was all black, and mostly Cocker Spaniel with floppy ears and a cut-off-tail. I believe Milo did the tail operation when Trousers was a very small puppy, because that is what you did with Cocker Spaniels. Trousers was a happy, playful puppy. He grew up to be my good buddy. Trousers had a good buddy, too.

Poppa bought a lamb that he brought home to raise into a grown sheep that would become a meat supply for the family. At first, we fed it from a baby bottle. Soon however it was grazing on the lawn, and at times got grain feed. It wore a dog collar. A light chain was fastened to the collar on one end and to a stake in the grass on the other end. When the grass was well mowed by the grazing lamb the stake would be pulled up and moved to another place on the lawn. None of our neighbors protested our having a lamb like they had when Father raised pigs. In fact, neighbor James Gross raised goats for milk and for meat. If the Gross family went on a trip, they sometimes asked us to care for the goats and to milk them. We could use the milk. I never liked the goat's milk that well. But we children had fun trying to squirt a warm stream of goat milk into each other's mouths when we milked the goats.

The lamb was in the yard where I often played with Trousers. The lamb and the dog got used to each other. In fact they learned to like each other, and would even sleep beside each other. They became best friends.

The lamb soon grew into a grown sheep. It was good that we never gave it a name because it was not to be a pet, but was to be eaten. Poppa would not butcher the sheep himself. So one day he took out the back seat of our old Model-A Ford. He then put the sheep in the back of the car and slowly drove out our rough rocky lane. Trousers saw his friend the sheep going away in the car, so he ran after the car. Poppa saw Trousers running along after him and the sheep, but thought that Trousers would soon give up and go back home.

When Poppa got out to the main road he saw that Trousers was still following. Then he started driving faster than Trousers could run, but he never knew what happened to the little sheep-loving dog. Trousers didn't come home that night. I missed him and became worried. He didn't come back the next day or the next. Trousers never came home again. We didn't know if he got lost, or got hit by a car or a truck. I missed him a lot and missed the sheep too.

In school we were permitted to do some woodcarving in art class. First, I carved a little duck out of red cedar wood. It turned out really well. Then I remembered Trousers, and decided to carve a little dog like him. The wood was light colored, but otherwise it looked much like I remembered Trousers. I made his one leg to hold up like an Irish setter pointing out a pheasant or other game bird. Trousers would do that sometimes. I never quite finished the carving to be smooth the way I had sanded the duck. It worked out okay because Trousers' hair was a little curly and rough looking. I colored it black on the computer and gave him a nose bump and an eye so you can see even better what Trousers looked like. I have another picture that I like best of the carving of Trouser where he is standing with the Good Shepherd who is holding a lamb. The shepherd carving was given to me as a token of appreciation by Immanuel Mennonite Church. I was their shepherd for a number of years. They also gave me a beautiful shepherd's staff made by David Nafziger from layers of oak wood glued together and bent into a wonderful crook at one end that could be used to catch straying sheep. Trousers, however, had no shepherd staff to catch him, but like a good sheep dog he stayed with his sheep as long as he could. Good-bye, good- bye Trousers. We will remember you as long as we can.

CHAPTER 11: *Snake in the School*

I was now in the third classroom at Park School for fifth, sixth and seventh graders. I was doing pretty well in school by now. Since I was a year older than many students in the same class I was beginning to look larger and become a leader. Still my favorite school times were recess and lunchtime. The school was next to Park Woods, a fun place to be and explore. The teachers let us do that, but it was usually David and I who would go into the woods at lunchtime. We would finish our lunches as quickly as we could, and then be off to look for wildlife in the woods. There were usually birds. I knew the names of most of the common ones. There were lots of squirrels and some rabbits. There were also snails and snakes, but no puppy dog tails that little boys are made of. You know that according to the nursery rhyme, don't you? The girls stayed out of the woods, which was fine with us.

We sometimes found little tadpoles in the wet weather creek that was a beginning branch of Blacks Run which flowed through Harrisonburg. There were also mosquitoes, which didn't bother us much. In stream pools we would see mosquito larvae. First they were what we called "wiggle tails." They would wiggle around in the water in what looked like an upside-down creature. They often stuck their tail right up to the top of the water. After a while they became reversed and more right side up. Now they had a fat head that was on top and a curved tail underneath. They looked something like a question mark. This stage was called a pupa. They didn't stay that way long, because a flying mosquito would soon emerge. I knew that butterfly caterpillars turned into a chrysalis. I had seen one kind hanging on milkweed leaves in late summer. They were a beautiful green color with golden spots that hung on a slender silky thread. They would slowly break open and a Monarch butterfly with orange-brown and black, folded wings would emerge. The butterfly would hang upside down for a long time until its wings unfolded and got stiff enough to fly. We learned that we should never try to speed this process along, because we would damage the delicate wings, and it might never be able to fly. I knew that moths made cocoons. Some large moth cocoons might look more like a rolled-up leaf covered with a silky web covering. In Japan moth caterpillars that feed on mulberry leaves spin webs that are harvested to make shiny soft silk cloth. Like butterflies, the moths eventually come out of their cocoons, unfurl their wings slowly and fly away into the night. All these processes of change were called metamorphosis, which I learned was a Greek word for change.

Humans didn't have metamorphism, or did we? I was "metamorphing" all the time. I hoped that some day the change would be so great that everyone would call me John, not Johnny. That did eventually happen, with the exception of one man, who was father's boss in the box room, who kept calling me Johnny.

When I was middle-aged and he was elderly, this man was in the Sunday school class that I taught. He still called me Johnny, and

I accepted it from him, but understood that whatever you called it, some things just didn't seem to have a metamorphosis.

I learned a lot of things from David, which he learned from his father who was a biologist. I also read books and guides to all kinds of creatures. David particularly liked snakes. As a young man, he even caught rattlesnakes with his bare hands. I never tried that trick, but I did catch other snakes. David became a biology teacher, very much like his father. He taught high school biology to our three children just like his father had taught me. Our boys, Tim and Theo, became skillful hunters like David, which was far better than I was as a hunter.

Now we are back again from the future. One day David and I were down in Park Woods at lunchtime. I saw a movement of something long and striped yellowish green and black. "David", I called. "I see a Garter Snake!" I spotted its head, with its forked tongue going in and out testing the air for odors. Quickly, I reached my hand down and caught it just behind the head so that it couldn't bite me. I held it up for David to see. It was a small one, only about eight or ten inches long. "Great," David said. "What are you going to do with it?" I reckoned that he would have been glad to take it home. But I had caught it and I decided that I would keep it. "What if I just put it in my pocket?" I asked. "That would probably work," David replied. "Snakes are usually quiet in a dark place," he said.

Just then the school bell rang and we had to hurry back to our classes. So I just put the snake in my pants pocket, and walked into the classroom and sat down at my desk. Miss Martin soon began our afternoon class, and I forgot all about the snake in my pocket. That is, until a girl raised her hand and said excitedly, "Miss Martin, there's a snake over at the wall." She pointed toward it. Everyone looked and some of the girls lifted their feet off the floor. I immediately saw that it was my little Garter Snake. The classroom turned into a chaos of chatter. Miss Martin said in an authoritative voice, "Is anyone responsible for that snake?" I sheepishly raised my hand. "John, catch it and take it outside immediately!" Miss Martin barked. By then the snake was slithering behind the piano. David helped me move the piano, and I caught the snake. I took it right outside, and let it get away. I wouldn't have a pet snake after all, and I was a little worried what punishment might follow when I returned to the classroom, so I went back into my classroom rather slowly. Miss Martin said to me, "John, stay after school and I will talk with you." Then she called the class to order and proceeded with the lesson.

I was still worried about the consequences, but kept quiet the rest of the afternoon. That was a good thing for me because I often got caught for talking too much with my buddies. I went forward to Miss Martin's desk to face my doom right after the last school bell rang and school was dismissed. Miss Martin, was not only my teacher, she was also the principal of the school and final arbiter of unusual punishments. I knew that mine was coming. It must be such an unpleasant experience that I have blocked it from my memory bank, because I don't recall it after all these years. I did learn that she was a reasonable person. My guess is that I had to stay in at lunch time for a while, and study or write sentences on the board instead of playing outside. In any case, I survived and passed on to the next grade at the end of the school year.

CHAPTER 12: *Passenger Pigeon/Dove/ Ivory Bill/Pileated Woodpecker*

I think that by now you already know that I love birds, but there are many more bird stories to come. I had become a bird watcher, learning to identify what I saw, and always trying to see new birds. Mourning Doves were common and I could identify them at a distance. I also read about their extinct cousins that were very common some years ago, and were larger than doves, and more colorful. These were the Passenger Pigeons. I saw pictures of them in books. I knew that they had been so common that they formed black clouds in the sky when they migrated. There were some rumors that they were still alive. Then there were the largest woodpeckers, the Pileated Woodpeckers, found in the mountains, and Ivory Bills that were likely extinct, but there were always rumors and claims that someone had seen an Ivory Bill in a great swamp. Both woodpeckers were black with red head crests. They both had some white plumage, but Ivory Bills had the most. I hoped that I might be able to find one of the "extinct" birds someday. How could a bird that was as plentiful as the passenger pigeon had been just disappear altogether? Perhaps there were some shy stragglers left hiding somewhere.

On the hill above us we had new neighbors, the Hostetter family. There were two sisters, Miriam and Pat, about my age, and a brother Doug whom I would play with sometimes. When their house was built there was heavy blasting because of all the limestone rocks they encountered when they were digging out the foundation. The blasters weren't very careful and rocks from the blast flew down the hill all the way to our house. In fact, one rock was so big it was like an old cannon ball. It broke the lath work around the bottom of our front porch. We didn't have a rock problem when we built our house, and the Shank family next to us didn't have much of a problem, either. I think that because we were near the bottom of the hill, the soil and clay that washed off the hill was deposited several feet deep over the limestone base rocks. On the hillside just north and west of us the land was pitted and scarred by erosion. Some gullies were so deep that when I explored them the top of the gully was over my head. This was a wasteland without cattle, but it did have plenty of rabbits. Sometimes I would see carloads of men who came from the city to hunt rabbits on this land.

As Doug got older, we played together more and more. Sometimes we would just lie in the grass and talk. We often talked about the war in Vietnam, and how the gorillas dug underground tunnels to hide from American solders. We were saddened by the war. We talked sometimes about digging an underground tunnel from my house to his. With our heavy clay soil and rocks we knew it would be an impossible task, but it was nice to think about the fun we could have in such a tunnel. Is it any surprise that when Doug grew up he went off to help the people of Vietnam just after the war? He became an expert on Vietnam and learned to speak the Vietnamese language. His sister, Pat, also spent several years there.

Back from the future again! I was writing about birds. Doug, Norman, David and I had set up a big board against a tree below Doug's house that we used as a sliding board. Now this is where the birds come into the story, as you will see. I was alone at the sliding board tree one afternoon when I decided to climb the tree and hide as best as I could among the leaves. I was as still and quiet as I could be. I wanted to see if any birds would come near me. After a long wait, a dove-like bird came and roosted so close to me that I could have reached out and touched it. I didn't move a finger or blink an eye, but just stared at the bird. It was grayish with a tint of rose color. The feathers of its neck sparkled a little like a humming bird or like starlings when I saw them up-close. The bird's shape was like that of a Mourning Dove, but it looked bigger. I had never seen a Mourning Dove that looked quite like this. Could it be a Passenger Pigeon, I wondered? It seemed almost pigeon-sized. After a while it flew away, but never seemed to have noticed me. Was it dumb like some people thought Passenger Pigeons were that they got killed off so easily? I climbed down the tree and ran home where I found all the Passenger Pigeon pictures and Mourning Dove pictures that I could locate. I looked and looked. Both birds looked about the same shape, but the Passenger Pigeon was easily the most colorful. The bird I had almost touched probably was not colorful enough or even large enough to be a Passenger Pigeon. Disappointed, I had to conclude that I had not found a Passenger Pigeon, but had seen only a Mourning Dove up-close in a way that I had never seen one before.

When I saw the first Pileated Woodpecker in Park Woods, I asked myself, "Could this be an Ivory Bill Woodpecker?" I was fairly sure the answer was no. However, I went home and checked the pictures carefully. The woodpecker I had seen didn't have white wing tips like an Ivory Bill. He had to be the more common Pileated Woodpecker. In any case, it was a beautiful bird, and when it pecked a tree it sounded like a bass drum.

CHAPTER 13: *Blue Bombers and the Hat*

One winter I counted 13 red male Cardinals in our backyard feeding on cracked corn that we had put out for the birds. Blue Birds lived in a big hole in a fence post near a farm lane. Later Sparrow Hawks (now officially called Kestrels) nested in the same hole. One summer a pair of Blue Jays built their nest not too high up in a big black locust tree along the fencerow at the edge of our backyard. One day while Norman and I were playing in the backyard I noticed the nest. "Norman," I said, "I think I'll try to shinny up the tree and see what is in the nest." "Great idea," said Norman. "I'll do it after you." So I started to climb the tree. It was hard work, but I was almost to the nest when I heard the parent Blue Jay scolding me. Suddenly, I was hit on the head by a feathered bolt of blue lightning! The parent had dive-bombed me and pecked me on the head. Whew! It hurt more than the first grade teacher's red ruby ring. I scrambled down the tree as fast as I could. "That bird really got me a good one," I told Norman. "I saw it," Norman said. "Does your head still hurt?" "Yes, indeed" I replied.

I wanted to outwit those birds and see into their nest. "I bet there are babies in the nest," I said to Norman. "I have a ball cap that I could put on," I said, "but I would still feel a hard peck even through the cloth." "I got an idea," Norman replied. "We have a big cone-shaped straw hat like some Chinese wear. I think that it would protect our heads." "Great," I said, "Why don't you run home and get it?"

Norman was gone only a few minutes. The hat had strings to tie under the chin to keep it on tight. "May I try it first?" I asked Norman. "Sure," he replied. So I put the hat on my head and tied it tight. Then I started up the tree again. This time both parents bombed me, but they just kind of glanced off the hat. I got to look into the nest. Sure enough there were baby blue jays in the nest. They were kind of naked except for a little dark fuzzy down. They didn't look at all like baby "pee-pees." They had big eyes and long necks. They craned their necks as high as they could, opened their big moths as wide as they could, and loudly chirped for food. They all seemed so hungry. I climbed down and told Norman what I had found. Then he climbed the tree with the protective hat. He wasn't bombed as hard as me. The blue jays were catching on that this didn't stop us. Norman also got to see the babies. We didn't disturb them again for a while. The next time we looked into the nest, the babies were much larger and were starting to get blue and white feathers. Again the Chinese hat protected us. After that, we left them alone, and they soon flew away from the nest.

CHAPTER 14: *Ghosts in the Chimney, Swoops in the Sky*

$\mathcal{I}$n the evenings we saw Chimney Swifts flying around catching mosquitoes and other insects. They were good birds to have around. If you watched closely, you could see them rapidly flapping their wings. In fact, they flapped so fast that it looked like one wing went down while the other one went up. I didn't know any other bird that looked like that. Really, though, scientists know that they flap both wings down together and up together like other birds. It is an optical illusion related to how our eyes perceive rapid motion. It was fun to sit out in the evening and watch the swifts flying about. As it got dark a group of swifts would swirl around together over a big wide chimney at the nearby college, and then suddenly all dive together and disappear. Then another group would do the same thing. Suddenly all the swifts were gone for the night.

Once we heard a fluttering and bumping sound in the chimney upstairs. The stovepipe hole had been covered for the summer with a metal plate, with a picture hung on it to look nice. Soon black soot was coming out of the chimney hole around the metal plate where the plate was not as tight as it should have been. What could this be? Was It ghosts in the chimney? Someone called Mother, and she came and opened the hole by removing the plate.

A confused bird flopped out. It was all covered with soot, and was making a big mess. One of the older children caught it, and took it outside. After a while it perked up and flew away. It was likely a Chimney Swift looking for a place to nest. But our chimney was too dirty with soot to be a nesting place. I don't think that it ever went into our chimney again.

Sometimes while we were watching birds in the evening we had a special treat. We would see Nighthawks flying among the Chimney Swifts. They were much larger than the swifts and flapped their wings slowly and erratically. They were dark gray with long pointy wings. They had white collars on their throats and each wing had a white stripe. Circling around, one would fly up really high and then go into a bombing dive even faster then the Blue Jays. At the end of the dive it would spread out its long wings to break the dive. The wings would seem to bow with the force, and there would be a sudden loud whirring, swishing sound. These were the male birds displaying their prowess to admiring females. After they paired off, the birds would hollow out nests in the gravel on the flat roof of the college administration building. At least once I climbed up on the roof and saw some Nighthawks fly away, but I didn't find a nest that time. I only read about how they nested.

CHAPTER 15: *To Raise a Mockingbird*

$\mathcal{W}$hen birds were nesting, we would sometimes find babies that had been pushed out of the nest before they could fly or escape from cats. Now I will tell you some stories about things we did that the law would never permit today. Some of these laws for protecting animals were made after I was grown up. Back then, we were somewhat isolated and didn't know about such laws. Someone in the family found a baby Mockingbird. It was feathered well enough that we knew what kind of bird it was, but it couldn't fly or defend itself. Someone decided that we should try to feed it and raise it until it could fly and fend for itself. I am quite sure that it wasn't I who started this project, but I helped as a younger sibling.

We fixed up a box for the bird and put it in our upstairs kitchen. We tried feeding it various things like bits of bread soaked in milk. We may have tried catching small insects for it. Whatever we did, it was always hungry, sticking up its little neck and opening its mouth and chirping pathetically. It would also poop a lot, and things around its box got messy. We were no match for its parents in bringing it good things to eat, and it soon died. We were very sad because we really wanted to help the bird, and not let it get eaten by a cat. Our best efforts were not enough, however, and we totally failed. We loved to listen to the mockingbirds sing, and hear how they mimicked other birds' calls. We learned that the best thing we could do was to leave them to care for their own babies.

Mockingbirds, like Blue Jays, can be quite feisty in defending their nest and young. They peck hard, as I found out years later when I accidentally walked near a nest on a neighboring farm. Both parents came after me, and I got out of their territory in a hurry. The baby Mockingbird that died was apparently separated from its parents and it would have died anyway. It would take an expert biologist to successfully raise a young Mockingbird. Today, it would be breaking songbird protection laws to try to do this at home like we did. I bet that you knew this, if you love birds the way I do.

A long time ago, I saw some wonderful pictures of Mockingbirds flying, and I drew them with a black ballpoint pen. My drawings turned out well enough that I kept them for many years. On my computer, I turned the drawings into a picture of Mockingbirds trying to drive a cat away from their nest area. You can find this picture in this book and think of how a Mockingbird is willing to risk its own life to defend its babies. You see, Mockingbirds are excellent parents, or there wouldn't be any Mockingbirds in our world today. Let's give a cheer for Mockingbird parents:

Who feeds its babies all day long? The Mockingbird,
The Mockingbird, Hooray! Hooray!
Who drives a stalking cat away? The Mockingbird,
The Mockingbird, Hooray! Hooray!
Let's give three cheers for the Mockingbird.
Hooray! Hooray! Hooray!

Chapter 16: *School Games and Stunts*

$\mathcal{W}$e played a lot of games at recess time, like Hide and Seek, Kick the Can, and Tag. I was pretty good at the games that we played, especially Red Rover. In Red Rover, you choose up two sides. Sometimes I was the captain and could choose strong and fast boys and girls. I always also chose some of the smaller kids that I could defend. Each side would line up holding hands on opposite sides of the school lawn. Then the side with the first turn would call out "Red Rover, Red Rover, send someone over." The other side would choose a strong runner who might be able to break through the opponents' line. If they did break through, they could bring back someone from the opponents' line to become part of their own line. If they couldn't break through, they had to join the opposite side.

One had to run hard and jump quickly at what looked like a weak link of hands to break through. I was big and fast enough to do this quite successfully, but there were others equally as good as I. We had great fun playing, and were always disappointed when the bell rang and we had to go in to our studies.

There were two brothers at school who were like clowns and circus acrobats. The main road running past the school had several long curves and ran downhill from the college campus to the school and beyond. These two boys would take their bikes up to the college campus and start down toward the school. They would lean forward on their bikes, putting their weight on the handlebars. Slowly they would raise their feet until they were on their bicycle seats. Then they would shift their weight to their feet, and stand straight up. Their bikes would roll faster and faster down the hill. They would put their arms out like wings, to help give them better balance control. Leaning a little one way or the other would cause the bikes to turn around the curves. We always were on the lookout for cars when they did this stunt, and no one ever got hurt. They would have to sit down again to put on the bicycle brakes because they had foot brakes on the back wheel, but no hand brakes. Do you think that you could do this trick? I don't know how they learned it, but it was something like riding a small skateboard with very big wheels. You shouldn't try this at home, and certainly not on a busy street today. I never did it. The two brothers moved away, and I never learned what happened to them.

Another boy, Harry, was always doing all kinds of things with wheels. Harry was older than I, but all of us were his friends. He got, or perhaps he made a unicycle. This has a bicycle seat, but only one wheel. Harry would ride it to school and all around Park View as though it were not difficult at all. I never learned to do this either. Harry became a builder and a painter. A friend once said that Harry had a special tool for every job. He didn't know of anyone else who had so many tools. Some of them Harry made himself. I assume he was the only one who knew how to use some of his tools. It is handy to develop special skills that are all your own. Can you do something that almost no one else can do?

CHAPTER 17: *Spelling for the Pond, Algebra for John*

$$X = 2Y + Z$$
$$C = \pi R^2$$
$$A = L \times W$$

*W*hen we walked the long way home from school, one of our favorite things to do was to visit the fishpond on the college campus. This was an historic spot on the campus. Sometimes some of the college students would throw each other into the pond. This happened especially to young men when they announced that they had gotten engaged. I think the young women usually missed out on this mischief at that time. My friends and I would stop by to see the fish amid the water lilies. In winter we could see the goldfish swimming under the ice. If the winter was extra cold, the water sometimes froze right down to the bottom, entrapping the goldfish. That didn't happen very often, but if it did, the fish seemed to be no worse off for their imprisonment when the ice finally thawed.

At times we would splash each other with the pond water, but we didn't try to push each other into the pond. Do you think that we were smarter or better behaved than the college students? We would also try to skate on the pond if it was frozen. Once, when I tried this, the ice broke and I plunged two feet to the bottom. I was totally soaked and freezing cold, but I had to walk all the way home that way. Boy, was I ever glad to be able to take off those wet clothes and get into dry ones!

I never liked spelling very well. In fact, you might say that I hated spelling. I don't think that I could distinguish sounds very well, and the rules seemed so difficult and inconsistent. Once after I got a bad report card, as usual, I stopped by the fishpond. It was a cold day, but there was no ice on the pond. I had my book-bag with me that held my spelling book. I told a friend, "I feel like just throwing my old spelling book into that pond." The friend said, "I bet you're afraid to do it! I dare you to do it." I pulled that offensive spelling book out of the bag, and tossed it right into the pond. Then I went on playing as if nothing had happened. My friend couldn't believe his eyes, but we were soon running around the campus, hiding behind bushes and jumping out to scare each other. Soon it was late and time to go home. My friend left, and I knew that I must also go home. What would happen if I came home without my spelling book, with a bad report card, and a note from the teacher that I should study my spelling lesson for tomorrow, and try to get a better grade? I wasn't eager to go home under those circumstances.

Begrudgingly, I walked over to the pond. There was the offending book. It was pretty well soaked, and only half floating in the water. I slowly bent over and pulled it out of the water. I shook the water off as well as I could. Then I tried to dry it a little better with my handkerchief. It was a sorry sight. I should have been a sorry boy, but I felt more fear of the consequences than I felt sorrow. I trudged home slowly with the damaged book in tow.

At home, I tried to dry the book better. It did finally get dry, but the pages were wrinkled and tended to stick together. I could still read most of the words in the spelling lessons. That is the way I used the book for the rest of the school year. I am sure that there were some questions about the appearance of the book. I may have said that I pulled it out of the pond without saying how it got into the pond. Of course, many of my friends knew what I had done. I'm sure my parents made me study spelling better than I had been, but I never got spanked for this. With more study, my grade may have improved a little, but I never became a good speller. It was a handicap when I tried to learn Morse code to use a ham radio. I never became proficient the way some of my friends did. I got into other hobbies, and stayed away from games that required spelling if I could. I'm very thankful for "spell check" on my computer today.

I got bored by my early arithmetic studies as well, but made passing grades. Finally, I found some math that I enjoyed and was better at than I had been at arithmetic. This started in sixth grade. Our classroom had fifth, sixth and seventh-grade students in it. We could all listen to other grades doing their review with the teacher. My ears perked up when the seventh grade started studying beginner algebra. There were interesting problems to solve, not just rote memorization. It seemed much more important than what I was doing in sixth grade math. Making equations with 'x' and 'y' just made sense to me. I soon found that I understood the subject better than some of the seventh graders. After that, I found math more interesting.

I took all the math classes I could in high school, and even tried to take a college math class when an older student got permission to do so. However, the director of my high school thought that I had no need for taking the college course. When I did get to college, my primary major was chemistry, but I took all of the math courses that I could work into my schedule. When I was a junior, the college algebra teacher had to miss one day of class. He asked me if I would teach the class for him. So, as a junior in college I got to teach other college students a subject that had woken up my brain for mathematics. Now since I may be boasting too much, I will make an honest confession. The summer after graduation from college, I enrolled in the biochemistry program at Virginia Tech. Just to fill out my schedule, I took a math course in an area of math that I had not studied so far. It felt like the memorizing arithmetic that I had not liked in grade school, and I got a "D" grade in that course. I didn't throw the course book in a fishpond, however.

Chapter 18: *To the Stars and Keeping the Planets on Track*

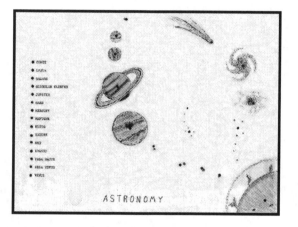

ASTRONOMY

M. T. Brackbill was a teacher at Eastern Mennonite which by now had become both a high school and a college, EMHS and EMC, in name as well as in fact. He taught many different subjects, led a choir that sang Christmas music, and gave a dramatic reading about Ebenezer Scrooge. Some called him a Renaissance man. But what I liked best was to hear him give planetarium lectures. He was a friend of Armand Spitz who had invented a low-cost planetarium, or star projector. M.T. Brackbill bought the first planetarium that Spitz built for EMC, and placed it in the dome of the observatory, which had been built earlier. We could hear him lecture about the stars and planets in public programs that attracted crowds of people. He seemed to know about the cutting-edge of science. He even suggested once that the earth might be several billions of years old, which was a shocking thing to a boy who thought the Bible said that the earth was created about six thousand years ago. M.T. Brackbill was my hero.

In sixth grade he came to my school to talk to the students about the stars. He showed us a star guide he had made. You could position it in such away as to see which stars would be visible at the hour of the night when you were star gazing. He had another chart that had what looked like two pens attached, with a little light bulb inside. One pen was attached to the base of the light. The stars' names were listed on one side of the chart with a little round metal head beside each one. The stars with these names also had little round metal heads beside them. He would touch the metal head for a star with one pen and also touch the metal head for the star's name with the other pen. If it was the right name for the star, the flashlight bulb would light up. So as you were learning the stars you could give yourself a little test and learn if you were right. He gave our teacher sets of two paper maps of the sky with stars and constellations that we could buy. One had names and one did not have names. I thought this was a great invention, and wanted to make one for myself.

Since I had not seen how M. T. had wired his star identification chart, I had to reinvent the wiring myself. I had wires, a flashlight bulb and a dry cell to test my ideas. It took me quite a while to come up with the right idea, but when I did, it all made good sense. Then I had to persuade Momma to part with some money so that I could buy a set of star charts.

After I got the set of charts, I took the one, which had the star names on the side, but none of the names listed by the stars and glued it to a thin piece of plywood. I then put little nails by each star's name along the side of the chart and another nail for each star that had a name. I could identify the stars from the other chart that had the names listed beside the stars. Then I needed lots of wire. In home construction in those days, there was often what we called "blasting wire" left over from setting off dynamite. It had colored plastic insulation, and was a thin, easily-bent wire. I collected lots of blasting wire. Each nail had to be wired to the battery or light. It took quite a bit of time to cut each piece of wire to the right length, then strip the ends of the wire of insulation, and finally to wrap the exposed wire ends to the correct connection point. I did all this work without adult supervision. None of my family or teachers would have known how to help me. When I was all finished, it worked like a charm. I soon learned the names and location of each star M. T. had identified on his chart. Then I could show friends or anyone else I could persuade to watch how the bulb lit up when I made the connection from the star to its name!

M. T. Brackbill also had built a small building on the top of the hill beside the observatory that he called Astral Hall. It was a place to give astronomy lectures, and a space for the Astral Society, a star-watching club, to meet. The club's motto was *Ad Astra*, Latin for "to the stars." There were all kinds of gadgets and lots of wires running about that building. M. T. also taught physics and liked to do many demonstrations. Although his star charts were as neatly hand-lettered as if they were machine printed letters, and meticulously organized, his wiring was the chaos of a mad scientist. The most amazing of his inventions was mounted on the ceiling.

This invention was a scale model of the solar system with planets that moved to show the different rates of speed at which they revolved around the sun. Each planet ball hung down from a model electric train engine that ran on a track that was suspended from the ceiling shaped like that of the planet's orbit. It was exciting when everything was turned on to run. Little Mercury whizzed around close to the Sun, then came Venus, next the Earth about the same size as Venus, each running at a slower speed.

After Earth was the red planet Mars with its southern polar ice cap. Mars took about twice as long as the Earth to go around the Sun. Then came giant Jupiter with bands of clouds and a big red spot. It went much slower than Mars. Next, yellow-banded Saturn with its wonderful tilted rings came creeping along, followed by the smaller Uranus and finally Neptune. Little Pluto was there to show its size, but on a true distance scale, it would have been out of the room. This was a "Magic Kingdom" to me as a boy.

CHAPTER 19: *To Elect the President*

*I*n the fall when I began seventh grade, Dwight Eisenhower was running for a first term as President. The whole upper classroom, fifth to seventh grades were to have a mock election and see which candidate we would elect. We were to campaign for different candidates, and then on election day we would count our ballots. The teacher would compile the results and tell us whom we had elected.

I didn't know very much about politics. I once overheard Momma say that her father said, "The Democrats spent a lot of money and messed up the economy, then the Republicans had to clean up the mess." However it was a Democrat, Franklin Roosevelt, who made it possible for Poppa to have a road construction job to help feed and clothe our family during the Great Depression. I doubt that Grandpa Brubaker ever voted in an election. My parents didn't vote, and seldom talked about politics. I often heard my barber complaining about President Truman, and he wanted to "get him out of there." Truman had decided not to run for another term. The Democrats nominated Adlai Stevenson to be their candidate, and the Republicans had war hero General Dwight Eisenhower as their man.

We studied a little about both major party candidates, but I sure didn't know very much about either one, and I suppose most of my classmates were in a similar situation. Even though this was a public school, most students were either Church of the Brethren, or Mennonites. We were "the quiet in the land," and didn't participate much in politics. Even most of the teachers were from these two denominations, and the principal, who was also my teacher, was a Mennonite.

I didn't have a clue about what I would do or how I would vote. I did see things about the campaign in the *Daily News Record*, the local newspaper. I knew that the candidates traveled around and gave speeches. They could be heard on the radio, but people didn't have TV's to watch the news. We only had black and white pictures in most magazines and newspapers. I did know that people supporting a candidate made signs and wore buttons supporting their candidate. The best-known slogan was "I Like Ike."

My friend, Don, who was in sixth grade, came to me with a proposal. "Let's support Stewart Hamblen for president." "Tell me about him," I said, "I never heard about him." "He's the Prohibition Party candidate. They want to outlaw the use and sale of alcoholic beverages like beer and wine." I knew that in the past there had been prohibition in our country. I also knew that mountain people in Virginia made their own "moonshine." We heard jokes about that. I learned that Stewart Hamblen was a popular musician who had been an alcoholic. He became a Christian and overcame his drinking problem. He made a good "poster boy" for the prohibition cause. I agreed to work with Don to get Park School to elect Stuart Hamblin instead of Eisenhower or Stevenson.

We took some of the cardboard circles out of jar tops to make round buttons saying "Stuart Hamblen for President." We recruited quite a few other boys and girls to help. The girls were good at making slogans and campaign buttons. Some other students campaigned for Eisenhower and Stevenson, which was likely the way their parents would vote. Some speeches were made. I was the principal speaker for the Hamblen side. I scolded my Mennonite and Brethren classmates about the evils of alcoholism. I said that we needed to get the "drunks off our streets." If we would elect Steward Hamblen, selling alcoholic drinks would be illegal again. There would be fewer problems with alcoholism. Our streets would be safer, and our country would be a better place. "So it is our civic duty to elect Stewart Hamblen!"

We completed our ballots. The teacher compiled our votes. Hamblen was the winner by a two-to-one margin. Our school campaign had worked. Of course, in reality, Eisenhower won the national election by a large margin and he became our President. In four years, when I was in high school, and Eisenhower was running for a second term, I got to see him in person when he flew into the Shenandoah Valley Airport. By then I was comfortable with his being President. I even learned that the Eisenhower brothers, Milton and Dwight, supported Messiah College in Pennsylvania, which was very similar to Eastern Mennonite College. Eisenhower's religious background was River Brethren or Brethren-in-Christ when he was growing up. This was similar to Mennonite, and stood for a peace position and against war. Eisenhower left this tradition to attend West Point, but sometimes his roots came out in some of his speeches. In 1953 Dwight D. Eisenhower said, " Every gun that is made, every warship launched, every rocket fired signifies, in the final sense, a theft from those who hunger and are not fed, those who are cold and are not clothed. This world in arms is not spending money alone. It is spending the sweat of its laborers, the genius of its scientists, and the hopes of its children." When you grow up and vote, I hope you know more than I did in 1952, but I do want you to vote your conscience.

Chapter 20: *SGA President Gets It on the Chin*

$\mathcal{I}$n seventh grade, I had the advantage of being bigger and perhaps more mature than some of the other students. A seventh grader was always chosen or appointed to work with the teachers and principal as president of the Student Government Association, SGA. There wasn't really a lot to do, or at least I don't remember it. Somehow, and I'm not quite sure whether students voted or I was appointed, I became the SGA President. I do believe I set a standard for other students to follow. I'm not sure about mine being a shining example, but you should learn the whole story first. It turned out to be an unusually trying year for many of us. I still think that we had a great classroom of students and I included a picture of us for you to see. Quite a number of us went to high school together, and some of us were even in college together.

Our trying year began when our classroom teacher and school principal, Miss Elsie Martin, got ill and couldn't continue teaching for the rest of the year. She must have had an experience something like I had in my first year of school. By the end of the year she was better, and she continued as a teacher for many years afterward. At first we thought that she would be back in a few days. We had a short-term substitute, who probably ended up staying with us a little longer than she had intended. She must have been eager to get on with her real life because we could sense that she just wasn't happy and neither were we. She quit before Miss Martin was able to return. Then we had a fill-in teacher for some time until a substitute was found for a longer term. By that time, many of the students were beginning to get restless, and a little confused about their lesson plans. We had several more teachers, but our situation was deteriorating.

A lot of things went on behind the backs of these temporary substitutes, and I don't think my example was helping much. I had always loved to whisper with my friends when the teacher wasn't paying attention. I had lots of ideas to talk about, and was likely using my nervous energy to make plans for outside of school activities. I really didn't mean to disturb the whole classroom! Several times I was caught talking too much and had to stay in and write on the board something along the lines of, "I must not talk except when asked to in class." I probably had to write it fifty or a hundred times before I could go out to play. I didn't, however throw spitballs, paper airplanes or try to trip up other students.

We must have had about our eighth or ninth substitute teacher before I got into really worse trouble. I believe the County School Superintendent must have had a problem finding substitutes for those troublesome students at Park School. Some of our substitutes were very young and inexperienced, but they were trying to earn a few extra bucks. They probably came with some trepidation about dealing with a classroom full of "Dennis the Menaces." We must have lived up to their expectations because they soon quit, and we had yet another temporary teacher.

Finally we got a teacher who was intent on laying down the law and making us behave. She soon caught me talking too much with the friends sitting close to me. "Johnny", she said in a stern voice, "Stop whispering! You're a bad example. You will have to stay in after lunch when the others go out to play." My whispering did stop until lunchtime, which wasn't too far away. After I finished eating, I stayed at my desk while the others went out to play. Lunch was our longest recess time, and I wanted very much to go outside and play. The Teacher just sat at her desk at the front of the room and looked at me, so I kind of looked down at the floor. It is possible that she may have been thinking about what she would really have liked to have done to me, but her better judgment won out. Finally she came back to my desk and said in a controlled voice, "John, you will have to put your head down on your desk for five minutes, and remember that you are not to whisper to friends." "Yes," I said meekly and put my head in my arms on the desk. Then she walked out of the room.

I suspect that she went to another classroom to talk with a more experienced teacher about what to do with me. I'm sure she had some things to say about our not being cooperative students. She was gone a long time. In fact it got to be so long that I felt my time should be up. I started counting seconds. I counted "one thousand one, one thousand two, one thousand three, one thousand four, one thousand five . . ." I knew that this would be about five seconds, and if you could count this far after you saw lightening until you heard thunder, the lightening was at least a mile away. I kept counting up to sixty, which I knew was a minute. I didn't have a watch, and my head was down and I was afraid to lift it up to see the clock since I might get caught peeking. I counted to sixty in this way at total of five times, and was sure my time was up. In fact, probably at least 10 minutes had gone by. I lifted my head and looked around. The teacher had not come back to tell me that I could now go out to play. Well, I just got up, walked out to the playground and joined my friends. Soon I saw the teacher running out of the school toward me. She grabbed me by the chin, twisted it until it hurt, and shook me.

Then she said, "You ought to be ashamed, you're the SGA President and you didn't obey me!" It hurt, and I was embarrassed at being treated this way in front of all my classmates. I wanted to explain, but knew that it would do no good, because she was so mad at me. She took me into the classroom and sat me down at my desk again. Then she went to her desk, but this time, she kept an eye on me. Soon the bell rang and all the students came back for their classes.

I am sure that I told my friends my side of the story, and I doubt that many of them thought that the teacher had been fair. But—soon we had another teacher. We must have had the reputation of being the worst group of students in the county. In any case, we kept getting new substitutes until Mrs. Sarah Miller became our fourteenth teacher of the year.

CHAPTER 21: *Fourteen Teachers and Only One Toot*

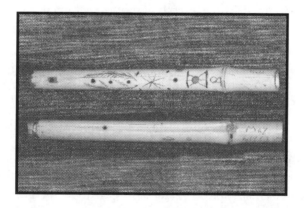

$\mathcal{S}$omething was different about Mrs. Miller from the beginning. She didn't seem to mind being our fourteenth teacher of the year. She didn't treat us like little rogues, either, and even acted like we were good students, and soon we were. She was more than up to the challenge, and even enjoyed it. Like Maria in "The Sound of Music" she became our leader, but was also one of us. She was very creative. She gave us extended time for art, and with my pencil, I drew the picture of a stallion standing on its hind feet like it was a king. In my picture, there were ducks on the lake. Geese were flying in the sky, but a "duck hawk" was about to catch one of them. An eagle was soaring over the mountains. This picture was my dream world, in which no teacher could disturb me. It won a prize in the county school art show. I'm including this picture for you to see. What would be your favorite imaginary world to draw?

Mrs. Miller also helped us to make shepherd pipes we could actually play tunes on. She brought hollow bamboo sticks to school. We cut them to the length that we wanted for our shepherd pipes. She showed us how to cut a square hole with one beveled edge on the end of the pipe. Then she helped us sand a cork to be the mouthpiece to blow across the beveled edge of the square hole. This would make a whistling sound of one clear note. Then we bored three small holes for the three fingers of our left hand and one underneath for our thumb, on the same side as the square hole but further down the pipe. Then we made three more holes for three fingers on the far end of the bamboo tube. We had made seven holes for the seven tones of the music scale. As she played the note for a key on the piano we would enlarge each hole until the whistle sounded that particular key. The lower notes were on the far end of the pipe. The first hole was a high "Do" when it was open and all the others were closed. The last hole was "Mi" when it was open, and a low "Do" when all of the holes were covered. The length of the tube to the hole that was open was the primary cause of the note that sounded. Then she taught us how to play several songs. We became a music band of pipers. We didn't try to lead anyone out of school like the "Pied Piper." We were enjoying school too much! Most of us were now eager to go to school each day. I'm including pictures of my shepherd's pipe for you to see. I used a wood-burning tool to decorate it "with some of my favorite things." Then I added the date it was finished, May 6, 1953, and my name. I thought Mrs. Miller was a great toot. She should have been named Teacher of the Year.

Miss Martin was able to come back as principal before the end of the school year, but Mrs. Miller continued to teach us to the end of that year. Somewhere along the line I must have salvaged my reputation as a good SGA President. Miss Martin sent me a note of congratulations for completing seventh grade. This little card has a 2-cent stamp on it, and is postmarked June 12, 1953. I went on to graduate to high school for eighth grade. The little card read, "To hope the future holds in store . . . All the things you want - - and

More. Congratulations." She wrote on the card, "Dear John, First I want to thank you for taking care of the note. Mrs. Miller said you did it very well. You have always been such a help to our group with your good thinking and balanced attitudes. My best wishes are surely with you. (Signed) Elsie A. Martin." I don't remember what the note was any more that I took care of, but I suppose that it was part of my duties as SGA President. Now I could hold my chin up.

I'm proud of all the students in our classroom that year. Our creative energy and intelligent minds had to be released and challenged. A good number of us graduated from high school and college. Some of us even acquired one or more graduate degrees. We became mommies and daddies, artists and teachers, musicians and college professors, businessmen and-women, pastors and administrators, lawyers and psychologists, farmers and diligent workers. We gave back to our communities as we had been given. Many of us feel deep gratitude to a great teacher and diligent principal. Some of us may even feel sorry for the dozen or so temporary teachers who failed to see or engage our potential.

Birds drawn as a child, carved as an adult.

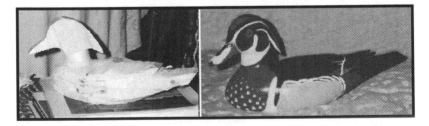

Mrs. Miller   Don   David

Miss Martin   John

Raymond   Lefty

Mary Ellen   Pat   Wendell   J Mark

John's class room and prize drawing.

SECTION 3: EARLY TEENS

CHAPTER 22: *Norman's Motors*

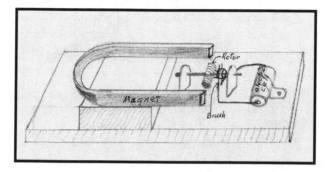

$\mathcal{I}$, and many of my friends, was now in eighth grade. My sister Sara didn't have to go to eighth grade. She was already in high school when it became a requirement to go to eighth grade. I did have to go to eighth grade, but it was counted as part of my high school program. The curriculum for eighth grade was just being developed. We had to study the usual subjects like English and math, but we also had science and business studies. Science class was one of my favorite classes. My friend David Mumaw's father, Homer, was our teacher. We studied about biology, electricity and other topics.

In classes about electricity we started learning how electric motors worked. One of the new students in the class was Norman Coffman. Like David and I, he already knew a lot about science, and he was a good student. He told the teacher that he had built several electric motors on his own. Homer Mumaw invited him to bring his motors to show the class.

I liked Norman and his motors. I was sure that I could do the same thing. So I went home and got out some finely coated copper wire. I always kept a good supply of it around. It came from old power supplies or other electric junk I collected. I had a table in my bedroom covered with this kind of thing. Mother didn't like my mess very well, but she knew better than to do anything about it except scold me sometimes. If our electric lights blinked or went out she would say, "Now John, what did you do?" Our electric wasn't always that stable, and sometimes a fuse blew for other reasons, and I had learned how to fix that as long as Poppa had a supply of fuses on hand. The electricity would usually come back on soon because the electric company had fixed something. Momma seemed to think that I had caused the problem and that I fixed it again, regardless of whether I had or hadn't.

So I had a number of old electric parts that I could use to make a motor. I also had a large horseshoe magnet. I wrapped two little pieces of sheet copper around a pencil. Then I made holes in them and connected one of them to one end of the copper wire from which I had scraped the insulation. Then I wrapped a metal bar with a hole in the middle with many layers of the wire. The end of that wire was then connected to the other half of the round piece of copper. A round piece of metal the size of a nail was pushed through the hole in what would become the rotating part of the motor. That created an electric magnet. I hollowed out a piece of pencil, fitted it over one end of the nail and glued it in place. Then the copper half circles were carefully glued to the pencil piece so that they did not quite touch each other, but made a ring of copper around the pencil. The spaces where the copper didn't touch were lined up with the poles of the electromagnet. I supported this whole contraption so that it could spin freely on the nail axis inside the poles of the horseshoe magnet.

I got a large dry cell (A dry cell is like a big flashlight battery.) and attached blasting wire to it to connect to the motor. The ends of the wire had its insulation scraped off. I was in a hurry to test the motor, so I held the wires in my hand for the time being. Later I would mount them permanently. I set the rotor (It is the part that turns.) of the motor at an angle to the poles of the horseshoe magnet. Then I gently touched the copper rings on each side of the piece of pencil with the uninsulated ends of the blasting wire which were connected to the dry cell. The little motor began to spin rapidly. It worked! Do you know why?

The moving part, or armature, of the motor had become an electric magnet. The opposite poles of this magnet were attracted to their opposites of the horseshoe magnet. But when the attracting poles were pulled close together, the wires came in touch with the opposite side of the split copper ring. Now the electricity flowed through the electromagnet in the opposite direction, causing it to repel, or push away the pole it had been attracted to. Since it was already past the pole of the horseshoe magnet, it continued to push the armature in the same direction until it was aligned with the opposite permanent magnetic pole. Now the current switched again and the motor kept spinning and spinning. Now that I had my little motor working, I mounted the connecting wires so that they were touching the split copper ring in the right way. I had a motor like Norman's that I could show to other people if they were interested, or if I could get their attention! I made several more motors before that class was over. In fact, Mr. Mumaw showed us how to make one with a round armature that had five separate electromagnets. It worked really well.

CHAPTER 23: *To Shoot or Not to Shoot*

$\mathcal{P}$oppa had told me stories about hunting rabbits with the small single-shot 22-rifle that he still had. It was dated from about 1913, which is when he would have been about fifteen years old. I don't remember that I ever saw him shoot the rifle, but I was getting the itch to use it. My friends David and Russell Mumaw were beginning to use guns on their farm. Groundhogs and rabbits were prime targets. Then my friend, David Messner, who lived on top of the hill above us, got his own 22-rifle. I really had to scratch that rifle-shooting itch! I finally was able to persuade Poppa to let me try his rifle. I bought a box of smaller 22-shells that we used to call "shorts." They were not as deadly as the "longs" that had more powder and lead. However, they were much better that shooting a B-B gun or an air rifle. I had a small B-B gun, but was never very successful hunting with it. I was told that a 22-rifle bullet could fly up to a mile, so I really had to be very careful in what direction I aimed to shoot.

Many birds were not protected when I was a boy. Pigeons, starlings, English sparrows, crows, hawks and vultures could be shot. I did a little better with the 22 than I had been able to do with the B-B gun. Starlings would flock to our garbage pile so they became one of my targets. One day, David Messner invited me to go across the hill from his house to shoot at vultures. Vultures apparently found updrafts along the hill that would help them soar high into the air. If they were just starting their flight, they might be quite low as they came over the hill. So one afternoon we climbed over the fence behind David's house and found a spot where we could sit on rocks partly hidden by small scrub-like cedar trees.

Several vultures came flying over the hill, but they were too high to shoot. Soon others came skimming over the hill. David got off a shot and it sounded like the bullet went ping through the vulture's wing feathers, but it didn't fall down or act wounded. Then I got to shoot, but nothing happened. We tried quite a while, but all we ever got were feather pings. Finally we gave up, as the vultures had moved on, perhaps frightened or scared away. We were no great hunters.

We came back to the top of the hill and started to look for arrowheads. We knew that they sometimes were to be found in the fields after the farmers plowed. There had been some house construction on the hill, and there was freshly exposed soil to check out. We had not been hunting for long, when to our surprise David found one. It was black in color, and had a good point, but part of it was chipped off at the back. I was not so lucky as to find anything, but David gave his arrowhead to me.

Sometimes I would go hunting for groundhogs in the field behind our house. If I was lucky I'd get in a shot, but I never killed any. Then one time I came across a large pile of chicken manure that had been dumped in the field. There was a hole in the manure pile that looked like a groundhog hole. I saw something moving at the hole. It didn't seem to be a groundhog. I walked closer to check it out. A mother dog and several puppies emerged from the hole. Apparently the mother, a stray dog, had dug a den in the soft manure as a safe place to have her puppies. The mother and the puppies were not afraid of me, and I got to pet them. I was really excited and I ran next door to Norman's house and told him. Then we went and looked at the puppies together. Neither of us had a dog at that time. We each found a puppy we wanted to keep, but they were still too small to take from their mother.

We each had to beg our parents to let us have a puppy. It wasn't too hard to persuade Poppa, since he was sorry about what had happened to Trousers when Trousers got lost or perhaps killed when following his sheep friend. Mother went along with the idea too. Norman was also successful in persuading his parents to let him have a puppy.

We watched them grow, and before long, they were running around and playing quite independently of their mother. They were already used to playing with us, so it was easy to finally take the ones we had chosen home to be our very own. I named mine Bowsers. It had some characteristics of a Beagle, but was really a mutt.

The neighbors weren't really pleased to have stray dogs in the neighborhood, but at that time we didn't have a dogcatcher to call about an unwanted stray dog. The mother seemed to have disappeared, but I found the last unwanted puppy out in the field when I was groundhog hunting. Somehow the thought crossed my mind that I could shoot it, as it was not wanted in the neighborhood. I hesitated. I wasn't really sure that I wanted to shoot Bowser's brother. Then I decided, well, it might as well be shot since no one was caring for it, and I didn't know what happened to the mother. I lifted my rifle and got the dog in my sights, then slowly pulled the trigger. There was a bang and a ping. The dog whimpered, took a step or two and fell over dead. My heart seemed to be up in my throat. I felt like slinking away and hiding. I don't believe I ever told anyone I shot a dog, but now I've told you. And you know what? I felt like a villain, not a hero. I never shot a dog again.

Sometime later, several of the Park View boys with guns decided to go crow hunting. We hiked north and east of Rt. 42 to a wooded hillside where we sometimes went to explore a small cave. We knew that there were often crows there, and sometimes men from the community went crow hunting in that area, as well. It was a good long hike on a warm Saturday afternoon. It felt good to be out in a "wild" area away from other people. The sky was blue with some puffy, white cumulus clouds. We could hear crows cawing in the distance. They were probably chasing some hawk from their crow paradise.

We were walking along in a grassy field that was not being used to pasture livestock. It may have been that deer came there to graze because it was right along the wooded hillside. It wasn't deer season, and we weren't hunting them with 22 rifles. Deer hunters usually use more powerful rifles.

As we were walking along I suddenly noticed some vultures soaring over. On the impulse I drew up my rifle and made an instinctive shot, hardly noticing where I pointed it. There was a bang followed by a ping. The vulture's wings went limp and it plummeted to the ground. We walked over to where it had fallen. The bird that had been so graceful soaring above our heads was now a rumpled black neck and an ugly naked, red head. Again, I didn't feel like a hero. It wasn't a skilled shot. It was simply a fluke that I hit it. I never shot at a vulture again.

We walked on to hunt for crows, but none of us got a chance at any shots. I had hit a big bird, but the whole experience was disappointing to me. I was more than glad to go home.

I still liked the idea of hunting, and continued to try for groundhogs without success. It was growing dark one evening as I was coming home from one of my hunting expeditions. I was still quite a distance from our house when I walked under a tree. Looking up, I noticed a dark object out on one of the tree limbs. I could not really tell what it was. I knew that sometimes groundhogs would climb trees. I finally concluded that it was a groundhog and could be shot. It wasn't too far above my head, but I could see only a black outline. I pointed the gun carefully and squeezed the trigger. Bang ker-smack! The creature hit the ground. I walked over to take a closer look at it. I could tell right away that it wasn't a groundhog. In fact, it was a cat. My heart sank. It was gray, tan, and white, a tri-color cat. It was our old faithful Pole Kitty. It was so old it had lost some of its teeth and wasn't able to hunt as well as it used to. Perhaps it was waiting for a bird to come and roost in the tree. Pole Kitty was certainly after something, but instead it became the hunting victim. I could not bear to tell anyone what I had done, especially not anyone in my family. I was learning a hard lesson about guns. One of my friends, I won't say who, had propped his 22 rifle on the projection of the sole of his leather boot in front of his toe. Somehow he had accidentally pulled the trigger. There was a neat half-round hole that just missed the front of his toes. To shoot or not to shoot, that is the question.

CHAPTER 24: *Spelunking Adventures*

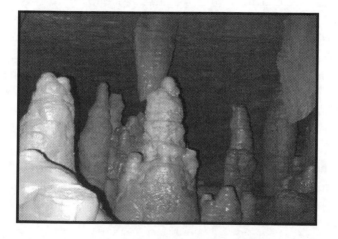

*W*e made a number of caving expeditions in the area where we went crow hunting. Momma was always quite concerned when I would ask to go with friends to explore a cave. Somehow I always finagled permission to go with the other boys, but she never failed to call out to me as I was leaving the house, "John, do be careful." I always thought that I was being careful. We made sure that we each had at least one flashlight so that if one went out we would still have some light to get out of the cave. We always went as a group of three or four boys together so that we would be able to help each other. Sometimes it was one of the Daves, or Lefty, or neighbor Norman.

The entrance to the cave was the first challenge. It seemed more like a large groundhog hole than the entrance to a cave. We tried to clean out the hole as well as we could. Still we each had to take turns squeezing through the entrance hole to get into the cave. Inside it was a fairly sizable room that we could all stand up and walk around in. There were a few stalactites hanging down from the cave ceiling. It was cool and damp, which felt really good on a hot summer day. When it was in the nineties outside, it was only fifty-four degrees Fahrenheit in the cave, like most other caves in our area. There were lots of caves or caverns in this part of the Shenandoah Valley.

I don't know how many other people knew about this cave, but we always seemed to have it to ourselves. Our flashlights seemed feeble shining on the dark, muddy, stone walls of the cave. The stalactites often seemed whiter and cleaner than the cave walls. The tip of each stalactite often had a drop of water hanging on it. It was a cool feeling to have a drop of the stalactite water fall on the back of your neck while stooping over to see something on the cave floor. The floor of the cave was often littered with rocks that had fallen from somewhere up higher in the cave. At places, a little stream of water trickled along the floor.

There were several other tight squeezes to get from one cave room to another. At the end of this cave, or at least as far as we could go, the cave wall was twenty feet or more in height. It looked like there could be another tunnel to explore if only we would climb the wall. One of our lights had gone out, probably a dead battery. I wanted to climb that wall and see what I could find, but I really couldn't see very well. It was almost straight up, and very muddy and slippery. I suspect that mud was being washed down along this wall from another opening on the hill above us that we had never found. There were a few rocky handholds. I grabbed onto a large rocky projection, when suddenly, it slipped free of the wall. I dropped to the cave floor standing on my feet, but the loose rock came crashing down on my toes. It hurt, but fortunately my foot had sunk so deep in the mud that nothing was broken. The mud had cushioned the impact of the big rock that came loose from the wall. That was the end of new exploration for that day. Our lights were getting dim anyway. So we walked, hobbled, crawled and squeezed until we were out in the light of day again. The warm sun felt good after being wet, muddy and chilled in the cave.

My foot was well enough to enjoy the hike home, but I was ready for one of Momma's good suppers when I finally got home. I had a lot of cleaning up to do before I was ready to gather with the family at the table. I suppose all the muddy laundry it made for Momma was another reason she didn't like my spelunking. I don't remember our table conversation, but I'm sure I didn't make one peep about the wall and rock falling adventure. I doubt my friends told their parents about it, either. But we all got home safely, and we were soon ready for another adventure.

West of the Mumaw farm was a much larger cave entrance. It was so large and deep and black that we called it the "Devil's Hole." We had to use a rope to climb down into it. There was an extended tunnel at the bottom, but it didn't amount to much more than the other cave, and I don't think there were as many stalactites or stalagmites in it. Perhaps other explorers had broken them off.

There was one significant feature of the Devil's Hole that really challenged us. High on the east wall, where we could not climb up, was another fairly large elliptical hole that we called the "keyhole." We could go above it on the steep hillside and look down. The hole was completely black. We could not see far into it. We could throw rocks from the top into the keyhole. We could hear them ricocheting off the walls for several seconds until they finally hit the bottom. We knew that it was really deep. It would have taken better ropes and climbing skills than we had at the time to get into it, so the mystery remained unsolved.

We continued to scheme and try things, but we never succeeded. We soon had explored the limits of the regular entry. Once when I was climbing up the rope out of the Devil's Hole, I noticed movement on the rock ledge in front of me. I yelled down to Dave, "I've found a little snake. It might be a pit viper." Rattlesnakes, Copperheads and Water Moccasins are the three pit vipers in Virginia, and they are all poisonous. Dave called up, "Are you sure that it has a triangular-shaped head?" I turned my flashlight beam on it again. It barely moved. I assumed it was too cold to have normal movement. I couldn't remember the color pattern well enough to distinguish which it was by that trait. I shone the light on the head. It certainly was triangular, not more elongated like a Milk Snake. I called back to Dave, "It has a pit viper's head. I think it's a Copperhead, but I think I can catch it."

It was only about six inches long and was only a baby. Still its bite would have been dangerous. I was near enough to the mouth of the cave that I could see the snake without my light. Dave soon caught up to me. I got a good foothold so that I could let go of the rope. I unscrewed the top of my flashlight. I took out the batteries and put them in my pocket. I then handed the open flashlight to Dave. He set it down in front of the snake, and I pushed the baby snake into the empty flashlight with a little stick that I had found. It was so sluggish that I had no difficulty getting it in. Dave then screwed the top of the flash light back on again with the snake inside. We finished our climb to the top with our little captive.

We hiked backed to Dave's farm. When we got to a good place to let the snake out where it could not get away, we opened the flashlight and gently let the snake slide out onto the ground. Dave agreed that it was a Copperhead. I knew that I would not be allowed to keep it at my house, so I offered it to Dave. He was glad to take it. By the time he grew up, Dave had become an expert in handling poisonous snakes. He is able to catch grown Rattlesnakes with his bare hands. This is a trick that I have never tried to do. This was just one more step along the way for Dave to become a high school biology teacher, just like his dad.

Chapter 25: *Frisky Foxes and a Confused Masked Bandit*

The Mumaw family found a number of interesting wild animal pets on their farm. One time Mr. Mumaw found a litter of Red Fox pups. A small wooden chicken house on the farm was adapted into being a home for the foxes. They could be fed much like puppies, and they became rather tame. They were always quite frisky. They would pounce on each other like foxes pounce on mice. Have you ever seen a fox pounce? There was playful fighting and biting, until some new attraction came along. The fox kits were good climbers, and it was good that the chicken house was a well-built building, or they would have soon found a way out.

They needed more exercise than they could get in this confined space. Mr. Mumaw built a treadmill for them to run on. It was a big wheel, three or four feet in diameter, made of wood and hardware cloth, which is a netting of wire soldered together. The foxes would jump into the wheel and run. As they ran, the wheel went faster and faster. The cubs seemed to really enjoy doing this. I'm sure all that exercise kept them fit and frisky.

They were growing up. It took a lot of dead chickens to feed them. They would need a better home. No one would welcome them running around loose on the farm, chasing chickens and guinea fowl.

So, Mr. Mumaw contacted the National Zoo in Washington. They were interested in taking the foxes and they were caged and transported to the Zoo. I wonder if you visit the National Zoo today and see Red Foxes whether any of them might be descendents of the Mumaw foxes. Maybe some of these foxes are even in other zoos as well.

Do you know what kind of animal I would call a masked bandit? Well, it's a Raccoon. David caught a little, about half-grown, raccoon that he kept in a small cage. It always had a bowl of water because in addition to drinking, it liked to wash its food. Raccoons like corn and can be quite destructive to a farmer's cornfield. I believe some farmers would say that Raccoons are corn-stealing bandits.

When David would put corn on the cob into the cage the raccoon would take the corn to its bowl of water. It would cup its front feet like little hands around the corn and lower it into the water, making a washing motion and rubbing the corn with its wet hands. After this ritual was finished, it would hold the corn in its front paws the same way we hold corn on the cob to eat. The Raccoon enjoyed its well-washed meal, prepared in good coon fashion, following good coon etiquette.

It also liked to play with ice cubes, but always found the ice to be a puzzle. It could wash the ice; even carry it around for a while. But soon, the ice kept melting until no solid ice was left. Then the poor Raccoon would search all around its cage looking for the lost ice cube. It never seemed to understand that ice turns into water.

A very puzzled and confused little bandit kept searching for the lost ice cube until it was given a new ice cube and could play the disappearing ice game all over again.

We had read the Craighead brothers' book "Hawks in the Hand" about falconry and wanted to try it. The Mumaw barn had a hole in the barn siding that led into an inner space between walls. A pair of "Sparrow Hawks" discovered the hidden space between the walls. These are the smallest falcons. They feed mostly on mice and grasshoppers, but occasionally will catch a small bird. They are good friends to have around the farm. The name was something of a misnomer, so it has been officially changed in bird books to the more scientific name, "Kestrel." So that is what I will call them now. These Kestrels made their nest in the barn wall.

It was hard to see in the hole because it was quite deep. However, it was possible to reach your hand and arm into the nest. A falcon has a sharp tooth-like projection at the end of its beak that is very useful for tearing meat from its kill. Let me tell you, if you stick your hand in the nest and an adult or grown young falcon is present, you may not forget the experience. Just ask Dave. Well, in any case, this was an opportunity for Dave to try falconry, and I would soon have the opportunity also.

CHAPTER 26: *Killy Killy and Rufus Red-tail*

The American Kestrel is a colorful and attractive bird. Both males and females have two black stripes or mustaches on either side of a white face. They both have blue-gray heads capped with a rufous-colored skullcap. Their backs and tails are rufous, barred with black. The female's wings are also rufous, but the males are blue-gray. Both have tan and some white with black bars on the breast. They have long, pointed wings and long tails. They can hover over one spot on rapidly beating wings as they search for prey in a grassy field. They are about the size of a Blue Jay. They nest in holes.

There was a gated lane leading to the farm to the east of us where now VMRC, Virginia Mennonite Retirement Community is. On one end of the gate was a large round post with a large nest hole. Sometimes Bluebirds occupied it, but the hole may have been a little over-sized for them. One summer, a pair of Kestrels took over the nesting site. It fitted their needs quite well, but also gave me the opportunity to acquire a nestling. I watched the nest in the post quite faithfully. When the eggs hatched both parents were kept busy supplying food for the young. I checked to see how they were growing. They were covered in white down, and soon showed signs of developing colored feathers. The best time to get a young falcon is when it is almost ready to fly. I chose a "chick" with slate blue wings marking it as a male. In many hawks the female is the largest of the pair, but for Kestrels there is little difference in size between the female and the male.

When the flight feathers on my chick were well developed, I took it from the nest. I had succeeded in getting it without getting into painful bites or scrapes with the parents. I took it home and put it in our little chicken house that we no longer used for chickens. I made leather jesses, or straps, for its legs from old leather shoestrings. I had a leather glove so that it could perch on my hand while I held it tight and yet not get painful jabs from its sharp talons. I made a perch for it to sit on, and it could also sit on windowsills. It soon was flying around inside the chicken house. I got plenty of meat from defective chicks at the hatchery for my Kestrel to eat. It grew strong and sleek, with good healthy feathers. It was a lot of work keeping it fed, but by now I knew quite well what it required to be healthy, and I was committed to keeping it that way.

Like its parents, it called a loud "killy-killy" when it was excited. So I named it "Killy-Killy." I did not make a hood to cover its eyes like some falcons wear, but I did make a lure to train it to fly back to me. The lure was a bundle of feathers with a weight tied to a long string. I could tie a small piece of meat to it. Killy-Killy naturally went after the meat lure when I swung it in a wide circle close to the ground. It would catch the lure and fall to the ground clutching it in its sharp falcon talons. Then it would tear up the meat and feast. I would walk up to Killy-Killy, catch the jesses with my gloved hand, then put my bare hand around Killy-Killy's body and set him on my gloved hand after he had eaten his treat. I also tried to teach him to come to a whistle, but I wasn't very successful at that. I let Killy-Killy fly about freely quite a bit. I didn't really want the mice or grasshoppers he was able to catch, so I never really used him as a hunting falcon.

Before the end of the summer, I removed the jesses from his legs. I still tried to get him to come to my lure. He was catching most of his own food now, and paid less and less attention to the lure. He was now totally free and soon I stopped trying to have him come to me. I have often wondered what his life's story became, but I don't know. I hope it was a normal falcon's life. Whenever I saw a male Kestrel in the fields around our house I wondered if it was "my" Killy-Killy.

The next summer, I took a female Kestrel from the nest in the post. I called her Rufus Red-tail. I raised her the same way I had raised and trained Killy-Killy. She too grew into a healthy adult, but then there was an accident that changed her life. One of her jess straps got caught when she was flying off her roost. The force of her flight suddenly stopped by the jess badly strained one of her legs. She could no longer roost on both legs in the normal way. Unlike Killy-Killy, she easily learned to respond to my whistle. She would flop down on my gloved hand to receive a piece of meat. She was very tame and bonded to me more than Killy-Killy had ever been. She was also dependent on me for food since she no longer had two good legs and talons with which to capture her own food. She became my pet flying around the yard. Her jesses were no longer needed. But then another unfortunate thing happened.

I had persuaded Poppa that we needed a fishpond in our back yard. Poppa seemed to take it as a challenge to build it. We dug a hole about five feet in diameter and about two feet deep. Then we used metal sheets to form the mold in which to pour concrete for the walls of the pond. We mixed the concrete a wheelbarrow load at a time, in a small, motorized mixer that Poppa rented or borrowed. As we poured in several loads of concrete, the metal walls began to bulge inward all around the pond. We had to hastily construct more inner wood supports for our walls. We were then able to finish mixing and pouring the walls. The inner walls seemed to be corrugated. At some spots, the wall was about four inches thick as we had intended, but at other places, it was five or more inches thick. I secretly hoped that friends who saw the wall thought that it had been designed this way.

After the walls hardened, we took out the bracing and the sheet metal form that had bulged. We leveled the ground at the bottom, and mixed and poured the concrete bottom for the pond. We smoothed it, but before it completely hardened, we scratched the name and birth date of each family member in the bottom. We let it cure, or dry, for what to me seemed like a long time before we tried to fill it with water. After it was full of water, we had to let it sit several days so that the chlorine used to purify our city water would evaporate. Too much chlorine would kill the fish. We knew that from having goldfish in a bowl in the house. We then stocked the pond with goldfish. This part worked quite well, and now we had a goldfish pond in our back yard.

Now you might wonder, what is the connection between Rufus Red-tail and the pond? One afternoon I was walking through the back yard when I saw Rufus Red-tail floating in the pond. She had drowned. Apparently she saw the fish swimming and dived down to try to catch one. She was not a Kingfisher, and never made it out again. I was sad about what happened and sorry that she could not have had a normal Kestrel life after living with me for a while. I loved it when she flew to my hand when I gave a special high shrill whistle. I missed her a lot. After that, I never again took another Kestrel nestling.

I did enjoy the fishpond. We started some water lilies as a nice addition to the pond. Then I caught a small green frog and also put it in the pond. It would sit on the lily leaves and catch passing insects. Then one day I found another strange thing in the pond. The frog was floating limp in the water as if it were dead, but in its mouth was a Blue Mud-dauber Wasp that had drowned. I surmised that the frog had caught the wasp and then gotten stung in the mouth. I knew that the wasps caught spiders, particularly black widows, and put them in their mud nests for the young wasp larvae to eat. You see, the wasp sting really just paralyzes the spiders and they are preserved in a comatose state to be eaten by the larvae. So I wondered whether the frog was really dead or whether it was only paralyzed.

I decided I would try to find out. I had a small microscope. I knew that one could see blood corpuscles moving in the veins of the webs of the frogs' back feet because the skin was so thin there. So I thought that if the frog was alive and I put the web of its foot under the microscope, I would be able to see the red corpuscles moving in the vein of the foot. I got my microscope ready and placed the frog's foot under the objective lens with a whetted cover slip on top of the foot and a microscope slide underneath. I moved the slide around slowly until I could focus the scope on a vein. It worked quite well with fairly low power and good light. Sure enough, as the vein came into focus I could see the red blood cells flowing in the vein. The frog was still alive, technically. Its little heart must still have been beating alright, but its nervous system could no longer move its other muscles to do normal frog things. It would eventually die. That big Blue Mud-dauber Wasp was a wrong choice for a frog's lunch. Nor could the wasp's sting save the wasp's life, because in the watery world of the frog, it drowned. Nature has some strange twists and turns, and this was a surprise ending. I still marvel at God's creation, but it doesn't always make sense to me.

Chapter 27: *Nasty Birds or Poor Keepers*

One early spring afternoon, we were out in the woods where we did spelunking and where I had shot the vulture. The air was crisp and invigorating. Most of a late March snow had melted, but there were a few patches of white among the trees. It was a good time to look for nesting hawks and crows. We saw a big bird fly out of a large tree ahead of us. It looked like a large owl, and it disappeared quickly and quietly among the trees of the woods. Way up in the tree was a large nest. "I think that bird was a Great Horned Owl." Dave said. "Could be," I replied, "it seemed much bigger than a crow or a Red-tailed Hawk." "It might be that the big nest is a Great Horned Owl nest," Dave added. "That would be a good climb up to the nest." "I don't think that I want to try it this afternoon," I told Dave. I was reluctant to tackle such a big climb, but I was also thinking about how the Blue Jays had attacked me when I climbed to their nest in our yard. What might a big owl do if we disturbed its nest? Also, I thought to myself, I never read anything about using an owl for falconry, so it probably wasn't worth climbing to the nest. "Aw, come on, John," Dave retorted, "I'd like to climb to the nest." "Okay," I said, "I'll be on the look-out to warn you if the parents return."

Dave shinnied up the big tree trunk until he could catch the first branch. Then he pulled himself up onto the branch. From there on, it was more like climbing a ladder. He worked his way up among the branches to the nest. The nest was so large that he had to back off from the tree trunk to get his head around the top of the nest. He climbed up another branch. Then he could look over the edge of the big pile of sticks that made up the nest and see what was in it. I was curious about what was there, but was also glad that it was Dave and not I in that spot just then. No big birds returned and Dave took a long, careful look. He called down, "There's one unhatched egg and two baby owlets. They're big babies, but they probably just hatched a day or two ago. I'm sure that they are Great Horned Owls." "Great," I said. "Good job. Now you had better get down before that mother owl finds you."

Dave came down carefully, but he was quite excited. "You know, I want to come back when the owlets are larger and we could take one and try to raise it." I agreed, but didn't know what kind of adventure we would be getting ourselves into if we took an owlet.

One Friday afternoon some weeks later, Dave caught up with me after class. "Hey John, he called out to me, "How about going out and checking on the owl nest this Saturday? My dad is coming in to school after lunch and I could ride along with him." So we arranged to meet, if our parents permitted. Saturday was a bright warm day. It was a great day for a hike. So we set out together. We had spotted some landmarks that we remembered to guide us to the right tree. We chatted together about how it might be to raise an owl. Dave said that he would take it first and then I could have it awhile. He had brought a gunnysack tied to a long string so that he could lower the baby owl in the sack and not risk dropping it to the ground. Dave always thought through details like that to make something work.

When we got to the right area of the field we spotted our landmarks, and knew that we needed to walk about fifty feet northeast into the woods to find the owl tree. We walked along without talking, trying not to make a sound. We wanted to get close before the parent owl spooked, so that we could get a good look at it. Sure enough, we spotted the nest in the tree and there was a big owl on the edge of the nest, feeding the babies. We waited quietly, trying to be invisible. The owl had not spotted us, but soon it flew away. I imagined that it needed to find food for its growing owlets.

Dave was eager to get up the tree. He thought that a baby that he had seen looked grown enough to take from the nest. He climbed to the nest without incident. "There are three babies," he called. "One looks like a runt compared to the other two. If I take a big owlet the runt will have a better chance." He reached in carefully and caught one of the owlets. Then he put it into the open gunnysack and pulled it tightly shut. He started down the tree, stepping down from branch to branch until he was sure the cord on the sack was long enough to lower it to the ground. Then he let the sack drop slowly down to me. He was soon on the ground beside me.

We opened the sack to see our new charge. It was all covered in downy white fuzz. But when it saw us it made a kind of hissing sound like it wanted to scare us away. It snapped its beak at us in a threatening way if we put a hand close to it. I knew it would be quite different raising an owlet from raising a Kestrel.

To make a long story short, Dave took it home and fed it for several weeks. One day he told me, "The owlet is a nasty guy to work with. He has really sharp talons you can feel through a leather glove, and it would take off a finger if my hand weren't protected. He eats and poops a lot, too. Do you want to take him a while, John?" I agreed, so on Saturday Dave brought him and I became an owl parent.

When I fed him I discovered that he could swallow a whole little "pee-pee" at one time. I had to keep a lot of little chicks on hand to satisfy his appetite. I got hurt a number of times by his beak and his talons even though I was always careful to wear thick leather gloves around him. He was a scruffy character, so the name "Gruffy" seemed to fit. I had him until most of his down was covered by feathers and he was flying around the little chicken house. I didn't think that I would be able to train him as I had the kestrels. He would be a night hunter, which would also complicate things.

Dave was willing to take him back, and I was relieved. He soon came to the same conclusion that I had. The owlet was too young to let go to fend for himself, but too big and nasty for us to keep feeding him. Dave decided that he would have to be killed. He would then stuff and mount him and give him to me to keep. I agreed. So I became the owner of a dead, stuffed Gruffy. Some of the neighborhood crow hunters learned that I had a stuffed owl. They thought this would be great to take hunting to attract the crows. I gave them permission to try it. Well, they took Gruffy hunting, but my stuffed owl never came back. They apologized and explained what had happened. I don't remember the details, which is just as well. That was poor Gruffy's sad end. It is possible to raise large owls and wildlife centers will do that for injured birds. But they are not ordinary pets. In fact, it would be illegal to do now what Dave and I did fifty years ago. We were not prepared or equipped to give Gruffy a good owl's life.

Sometime later, we were hiking and planned to go camping on Round Hill not too far from Dave's place. As we went along, we saw what looked like a big white rabbit disappear under a big rock. When we got close enough, we saw that it was not a rabbit but a downy bird the size of a rabbit. It had an ugly naked head. It was a baby Turkey Vulture. When Dave caught it, it regurgitated and made a stinky mess. We decided we would keep it anyhow, so we tethered it with some twine tied to one of its legs. Then we set up our camp for the night at some distance from the vulture. It still hissed at us and puked until it had nothing more to throw up.

Dave took it home and tried to raise it, but it continued to puke everything he gave it. He finally gave up, and took it back to the nest. Persons who have studied these kinds of birds have had to carefully develop techniques for feeding them. The California

Condor is a bigger cousin of our Turkey and Black Vultures, which has been brought back from the edge of extinction by hatching eggs and raising the babies by hand. The handlers use gloves that are like puppet heads of the parents when they feed the young and it has worked successfully. We didn't know anything about this, and this way of feeding had not been developed when we had the baby vulture. We were poor keepers and failed with both the owl and the vulture. I don't think that you would want to try this at home, even if it were legal today.

CHAPTER 28: *Conscience and the Stolen Lock*

*N*ow that I was in high School I was also on the college campus. The college and the high school were on the same campus and the high school used some of the same buildings as the college students and even had some of the same teachers. Since this was a Mennonite school and college, we had to go to chapel every day. High school students intermingled with college students for chapel. In fact, we were seated alphabetically by last name. If I remember correctly, boys sat on one side of the chapel and girls sat on the other side. There were big white attendance cards to fill out every day by the person on the end of a row. If you missed too often there were penalties, and tardiness could also be penalized. There were lots of rules to keep in general. For example, girls and boys were not permitted to hold hands. Some couples took short sticks and held their hands on the stick so that they touched. Well, students have no such rules today in either the high school or the college, which is now a university. I think that is a good thing because just following rules doesn't change how one really thinks and feels about something.

Chapel was a time for lots of admonition for good behavior, and there is some value in that. It helped us think seriously about our lives. We were also taught the gospel of salvation by grace and not by works, but works seemed to get the bigger emphasis. I certainly knew that it was wrong to steal, and I didn't want to be a thief. But this story tells you a little about how things worked out in my life.

One late afternoon I was walking across campus, likely on the way home. No one else was around at the time. As I walked by one of the large shrubbery bushes I spotted an opened padlock lying on the ground. For some reason I really wanted a padlock, but I didn't have much to lock up except my bicycle. I didn't know how I would use that lock on the bicycle, because it wasn't a bicycle type of lock. But I really wanted the lock anyway. It really didn't make any sense because there was no key with the lock. If I pushed it closed I would not be able to open it again.

I looked at the lock long and hard. I supposed that one of the school maintenance men had dropped it. It wasn't mine and it probably belonged to the school. It wasn't even useful to me, because I didn't have the key. I looked and I took. It went into my pocket, and I walked home. I put it away among some other odds and ends that I treasured.

For a little while life seemed normal. Once in a while the thought kept popping into my mind that I had stolen that lock. I tried to ignore it, but I began to feel worse and worse. Why had I been a thief? What made me do such a thing? What would other people think if they knew what I had done? These thoughts kept going round and round in my head. I felt worse and worse. Finally I felt so badly that I took the lock out of the treasure box, slipped it into my pocket and walked over to the campus. When no one was looking, I threw the lock into a shrubbery bush. I walked back home.

The trouble was, I just didn't feel any better. The lock still haunted me. Or was it my conscience speaking? I had stolen, but I had not confessed or made restitution. I fought this battle for some time, but finally decided that I needed to go to the Director of the High School's office and tell it all and make it right. I don't know if I prayed about it or not. I probably felt too guilty to pray. I just seemed to know what I should do, and didn't question what it was God wanted me to do.

Finally I did what I knew I had to do. The Director, Harold Lehman, was in his office when I knocked on the door to get his attention. I'm sure that he could see that I was quite nervous. I finally was able to get the story out, and the accepting way that he listened, helped me to finish my story. Finally I asked what I could do to make it right. He thanked me for coming in to tell him what I had done. He sat thoughtfully for a minute and then said, "I don't exactly know what the lock might have been worth, but I believe that $3.00 would likely cover its cost." I told him that I would bring him the money as soon as I could.

I don't remember if I had that much money or not, or how I got it. It was a lot of money to me at that time. I do remember that I felt like I was floating on air. I just felt deep peace where there had been complete turmoil and pain. Not physical pain, but emotional pain. Now the pain was gone. I had been a prisoner, but now I was free. I paid the money, as I had said that I would. The whole incident soon left my mind as I got into many other things, things that I enjoyed doing. It never bothered me again. I was forgiven. Sometimes I did remember that my conscience had spoken, and that I was free, when I obeyed its voice.

CHAPTER 29: *Dragonfly Pond*

$\mathcal{A}$ ll kinds of insects intrigued me, not just the fireflies that we could catch on our lawn on a warm summer evening. Moths, dragonflies, butterflies, beetles, bugs and whatnot caught my attention. Even when I was quite small, I wanted a butterfly net like one of my older brother who was studying high school biology had. I soon learned the technique of preparing an insect collection. I learned some from my older sibling, but also a lot from David Mumaw. At the time Dr. D. Ralph Hostetter and David's father, Homer Mumaw, were developing the college museum. Mr. Mumaw was preparing the museum's insect collection. Sometimes he would take David and me along, and show us some addition to the collection. David and Russell even helped him to collect some specimens for the collection.

I learned how to make a simple poison jar to put butterflies or moths into so that they would die quickly before they flapped too many colorful scales off their wings. The biology student's jars were made with cyanide pellets embedded in plaster at the bottom of the jar. This worked very quickly, but was too dangerous for me. However, a sheet or two of blotting paper cut into round pieces, soaked in alcohol and placed at the bottom of a pint jar worked quite well. I probably learned this from David. If it stopped being effective you could just pour in a little more alcohol and it would work again. You did have to be careful not to get too much alcohol or it would wet the wings and take away some of their beauty.

Somehow my brother Omar had gotten a Giant Water Bug for his collection. Mr. Mumaw also had one for the museum collection. Another thing in the museum collection that seemed to me to be a real prize was a big Hercules Beetle. It was kind of pale blue-green in color and had two horns on the top of the head, but in rows up and down, not horizontal like a bull. The many kinds of dragonflies also got my attention. I loved to watch a dragonfly fly about like a little helicopter. Flight of any kind appealed to me. I thought of becoming a pilot, even though I had never even gotten to ride in an airplane.

There was a little stream across the hill to the west of our house. It flowed in a little valley between two hills. Sometimes it ran fast and had small dams that made little ponds. This was a good place for finding unusual insects, but there were no real fish; only crayfish that looked like little lobsters. We liked catching them and bringing them home in jars of water. There were no big ponds in the little stream at the time, but one spring that changed.

There was a late, big wet snow that melted quickly and caused some flooding. There continued to be many good rains all spring. Once when we were hiking far afield, we crossed over the next hill beyond the stream and to the south. In the valley at the bottom of that hill there was a natural bowl in the pasture next to a small woods. There were no cattle in the field. It was a quiet, private place. That spring the pasture had become a sizable pond of water. Unlike most farm ponds with clay bottoms, this water was fresh and clear. The day was quite warm and to our surprise the water felt warm too. We soon were wading up to our knees, but knew that the water was deeper even though we could see green grass on the bottom. We walked back out of the water and stripped out of our clothing to go skinny-dipping. I had never swum in a public swimming pool, only in farm ponds, streams or small rivers. Poppa liked to swim. He had grown up close to the big Susquehanna River, but Momma was afraid of water. It was really special when Poppa took just us boys, no girls, swimming. This spring pond was easily three feet deep and we had a lot of fun swimming.

I think it was probably Norman Shank, David Suter, the closest neighbor boys, and I who were swimming at the pond that day. We often hiked around together, even though they were a lot younger than I was. I was kind of the Pied Piper to the younger boys on the north end of Park View. We always found plenty of exciting things to do. We had to dry in the sun awhile before we got back into our clothes.

Once we were done swimming, I had time to check out the insect activity around the pond. Dragonflies and damselflies were skimming above the water. I had never seen so many kinds of dragonflies at the same place. We all wanted to come back again, so we planned an expedition for the next Saturday.

I was planning to add a lot of dragonflies to my insect collection. I was no longer using poison jars to kill insects. Somewhere I had acquired a small syringe with a very sharp small needle. I would fill it with alcohol, and when I caught an insect, I could inject the thorax, or middle of the body, with a drop of alcohol. It was dead in an instant without any flapping of its wings as it did in the alcohol poison jar.

The next Saturday I was equipped with a backpack of things to kill and collect dragonflies. I also had a butterfly net, as did Norman and David. When we got to the pond it was swarming with dragonflies.

There were Green Darners and Blue Darners (the largest kinds of dragon flies), Ten Spots and Five Spots, medium sized, and little Amber Wings. The pond seemed like a training field for all kinds of miniature helicopters. One of my tools was a good insect book, and that is how I knew what I was seeing. We had to run around the edges of the pond to do our collecting. I soon had many samples of these and others I had not yet identified. After a good long time of collecting insects, we were hot and sweaty. It was time for a good dip. This time we had brought swim trunks and towels. We didn't need to skinny-dip or dry off in the sun. That day we went home tired and happy. It had been a great day. The pond slowly disappeared over the coming weeks, and after while, it all seemed almost like a dream. I never found the field flooded in the same way again. I did have a great dragonfly collection to prove that it had been real.

CHAPTER 30: *Butterfly Thistle Haven*

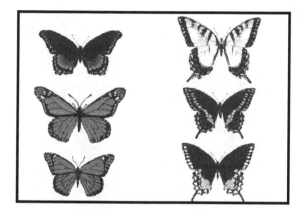

I knew that I was making an insect collection that would be tops when David and I finally got to biology class in high school. David would have a topnotch collection too. Probably my dragonflies would be my best collection, but I wanted a good butterfly and moth collection as well. I had an advantage in collecting moths because I could collect some of the big ones that came out of the woods when we had evening meetings at Morning View Church. Some of the finest moths I caught were the Cecropia Moth, Polyphemus Moth, Royal Walnut Moth, Imperial Moth, Io Moth and the pale-green-tailed Luna Moth.

I still needed a place to catch a good variety of butterflies. The small, white Cabbage Butterflies and yellow Sulfur Butterflies were common around our garden and yard. Occasionally I would see the large Tiger Swallowtails in the woods around Morning View, but

I wasn't able to catch them flying high among the trees. In early spring, I had found a Morning Cloak Butterfly in Park Woods and I also caught Red-Spotted Purple Butterflies around some mud puddles. Sometimes Black Swallowtails came to my mother's flower garden. But what I wanted was to find a butterfly paradise the way I had found a dragonfly paradise.

I had learned to make various kinds of display, or spreading boards for dragonflies, moths and butterflies. I had bought insect pins to mount them correctly. The butterflies and moths had to have their wings spread so that the lower edge of the larger upper wing would be horizontal. The lower wings had to be brought up as well until they tucked under the upper wings just a little bit. This way the colorful wing patterns were displayed at their best. The wings had to be held in place with paper and pins until they dried. Insect pins were stuck in the middle of the thorax at the right height for them to be displayed later.

We went to drugstores and collected empty cigar boxes to put our collections in for safekeeping. Each insect needed to be labeled with its correct name. We also put mothballs in the boxes to keep them from being eaten by small pest insects. The lids could be closed over each box to protect the contents when not being displayed. I had boxes of dragonflies, bugs, beetles, moths, butterflies, wasps and bees. I ended up with a large collection of cigar boxes that I kept safe for many years. Eventually, I donated them to Johnstown Mennonite School where I taught science and math for several years for their biology classes. But, this is getting ahead of the story. Now I needed a good place to catch butterflies.

I kept searching the fields and woods around our house, but I hadn't found what I was looking for yet. Then one day, I hiked farther north, to the Harmon farm. Sometimes there were beef cattle in the fields, but not that day. What I found instead were fields of deep grass with large patches of thistles. The field had not been grazed or mowed for hay. There were Canadian Thistles and big Bull Thistles in abundance, along with patches of milkweed. Along the fence row to the west were large trees of various kinds, including Sassafras Trees. This was the butterfly paradise that I had been looking for!

Many of the thistles were blooming with attractive reddish-purple flowers. Some of the thistles were already covered with white fluffy puffs of parachuted seeds, something like dandelion seeds. Some of these were being blown about in a light breeze, spreading the thistles far and wide. It was indeed a paradise for a boy searching for butterflies, even though it was likely a farmer's nightmare.

I returned to this field many times and greatly expanded my butterfly collection. Sometimes Norman Shank or David Suter would go with me and they made up their own collections. David Mumaw did most of his collecting on the farm he lived on. When one of David Suter's cousins came to visit from Pennsylvania, he went along on one of our expeditions to catch butterflies. Like me, he would soon be required to make a collection for his high school biology class. He apparently got a good head start on his butterfly collection that day. Many years later, when attending his aunt Grace's funeral, he sought me out and reminded me of the great time we had had collecting butterflies in Thistle Haven. He had gone home and he made a collection of his own for which he received an A grade.

So what kinds of butterflies did we catch? There were Monarch Butterflies on the milkweed near the thistles, but they also gathered nectar from the thistles. There were the little imitations of the Monarch called Viceroy Butterflies. Apparently Monarchs are not as appealing to birds' taste buds, but Viceroys were. The birds are fooled by the Viceroys' appearance, because if they eat a Monarch, they will not later catch a Viceroy, which, although smaller, still looks like a Monarch. We also caught Regal Fritillary and Great-Spangled Fritillary butterflies that looked very similar to each other. These are all brownish orange butterflies.

We caught many different swallowtails, large yellow and black Tiger Swallowtails, Spicebush Swallowtails that are black with bluish green patches on their lower wings and have caterpillars that feed on Sassafras, Black Swallowtails, and rare Pipevine Swallowtails with blue metallic-looking lower wings. We also caught smaller butterflies like Red Admirals, Question Marks, Buckeyes, Painted Ladies, and tiny Coppers, Skippers and Blues. We also found sphinx moths that looked like small hummingbirds. There are others I have not named, but in any case, they made for a wonderful collection. I too got an A, as did David; actually it was probably an A+. However, we did it for the fun of it and hardly thought about a grade.

CHAPTER 31: *The Prize Chemistry Set*

George Brenneman had a large Gilbert chemistry set with which he was able to do all kinds of intriguing experiments. George even had his own little shed set apart from their new house in which to do his chemistry experiments. I must have begged for a chemistry set, because one Christmas I received a small one as a gift. My little set had about two dozen different chemicals in little glass jars with corks on them. George's big set may have had around 100 different chemicals. I couldn't do all that George could do, but I could entertain my friends, and myself and learn chemistry. I learned that litmus paper turned blue in a base solution such as household ammonia. Acid solutions such as vinegar and lemon juice turned litmus paper red. I learned that magnesium, or Mg, as it was called by its chemical name, was a metal something like aluminum, which was called Al. If you lit it with a match, it would burn with a very bright blue-white flame. In fact, in the early days of photography, photographers used to burn magnesium to take flash pictures.

One of my friends, Raymond Brunk, came to my house to play one day. He enjoyed the things that I could show him with my little chemistry set. I had an alcohol burner that had a hot flame that I could use to soften and then bend glass tubing. So I showed Raymond things that I could make by heating and bending glass. I could make the glass very soft then pull it out into a tiny thin tube the thickness of hair. But what Raymond liked best and remembered many years later was taking iron filings, iron made into a powder, and sprinkling it into the burner. The tiny pieces of iron burned like 4th of July sparklers. I was learning that many metals can burn under the right conditions. By burning, the metal combined with oxygen in the air to make a metal oxide. A metal oxide dissolved in water made hydroxide ions which turned litmus paper blue, because it was a base solution. I learned later that another common household metal made excellent fuses for rockets when it burned.

George Brenneman apparently learned that I liked doing things with chemistry, just like he did. When he got older and no longer played with his chemistry set, he gave it to me. Now I had a really big chemistry set and could do many more experiments. I also learned that I could buy some of the chemicals at the local drug store. I learned how to make things such as gunpowder. This could be used in fireworks or to make rockets fly. I also learned how to generate hydrogen gas, which is lighter than air. Balloons filled with hydrogen will float upward through the air even better than the helium-filled balloons you can buy in the store.

CHAPTER 32: *Balloons Bursting in Air*

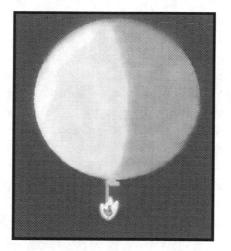

$\mathcal{M}$omma canned fruits and vegetables in glass quart jars. The jar tops were made of zinc which did not rust. Sometimes she made laundry soap from animal fat by cooking it with lye. Lye is a form of sodium hydroxide. It's important not to get lye on your skin because the skin will dissolve and eat away at the fat beneath your skin. I soon found out that lye and zinc mixed with a little water was a great way to generate hydrogen gas. So between my mother's canning, and her soap making, I knew where I could get the ingredients for filling hydrogen balloons.

Several of my friends would come over to my house to fill our balloons with hydrogen. We would use a soda bottle made of glass, usually a large one with a long neck, as the reaction chamber for our hydrogen generation. We would cut the zinc canning jar lids into small strips so that we could drop them into the bottle. The next step was to dissolve some lye in water, pour the solution into the bottle and quickly stretch a balloon over the mouth of the bottle. The reaction mixture would begin to fizz with hydrogen bubbles. If we had too little water in our mixture, it would get very hot, even boiling hot, sending steam and hydrogen into the balloon. This was not good. So we discovered that it was better to use a big bottle rather than a small one because that made it less likely that the hot lye water would boil up into the balloon. Sometimes the glass bottle got hot so quickly that the glass would break and all the corrosive mixture would pour out onto the ground. So we needed to work on a safe spot of ground that could be washed down. If it worked just right, we could quickly fill one or two small balloons with hydrogen. We would tie them shut with string and let them float up into the air.

Sometimes we even tied a message with our names and addresses to the balloon, with the hope that someone would find the balloon and send us a note. We never were lucky enough to get a response. It was fun to just stand and watch our creations disappear into the sky. This is what I think of when I imagine how it looked to the disciples to see Jesus ascend into heaven. Yes, and like the disciples, sometimes a cloud took the vision out of our sight. We also, would stand a while, staring into the heavens hoping we might get another glimpse.

One time, I had the brainy idea of trying our balloon release at night, or at least after it had started getting pretty dark. I would add a fuse that would burn up to the balloon and eventually make it explode. So I bought a big balloon to make it a more exciting sight when it exploded. I got the zinc lids and cut them into strips to drop into the bottle. I got as big a bottle as I could find and also got water and lye ready. There was a slight breeze from the north that would carry the balloon over open fields toward our next neighbor's house and the college and high school campus beyond. It was summer so not many students were around.

That evening several friends came over to my house around the time it was getting dark. We had some flashlights to help us see what we were doing. We worked on my front lawn. I added the chemical ingredients to the pop bottle jar and stretched the balloon over the mouth of the bottle. It was a larger than usual amount of zinc and lye, and the balloon filled up to a nice size. It was quickly fizzing hot and expanding rapidly. Some of the lye water bubbled up into the balloon but then trickled down again. Then the fizzing slowed and stopped as the zinc completed its reaction and dissolved fully. After waiting a couple of minutes until the reaction stopped and the liquid trickled down from the balloon into the bottle. I tied the balloon shut and removed it from the bottle. I had treated a piece of string with chemicals to turn it into a fuse. The balloon was nice-sized and it had a good upward tug from being lighter than air.

I lit the end of the fuse and let the balloon go to disappear into the night sky. We couldn't see the balloon itself for very long because it was too dark, but the fuse gave a nice light that gradually became like a very bright twinkling star. It went up and south toward the school campus, but we could only guess about how far away it really was. It seemed that we were watching for a long time, but it was probably just a few minutes. Suddenly there was a big bursting flash of yellow and orange light as the fuse fire ignited the balloon. A second or two after we saw the explosion, we heard a small boom, not quite as loud as a firecracker would have been. It was more of a puff. Our experiment had worked quite well!

We never heard that anyone else had seen our experiment. If they had, I still wonder what they would have thought it was. One college professor was quite interested in flying saucers. He investigated several stories of sightings. The one I had heard the most about sounded like the man who told it had likely been drunk. The professor could not find any other evidence for the man's story. Some persons who might have seen our little experiment may not have been willing to tell what they saw because others might wonder if they had had an illusion or were perhaps even drunk. I doubt that anyone but those of us who did this trick could really have figured out what actually happened. What would you have thought if you had seen what looked like a twinkling star moving slowly in the night sky, suddenly turning into a big ball of fire?

I used to draw pictures of flying saucers, rockets, as well as birds on the inside covers of some of my grade school books, but I don't think I believed that flying saucers were real, or that they were spaceships with people in them from another planet. I did think that maybe the air force had some experimental aircraft they might be testing which some people may have thought were flying saucers.

CHAPTER 33: *Rockets, Fuel and Fuses*

I had started reading science fiction about rocket trips to the
moon and other space travel adventures. I could get these
books at the public library. I got so involved in the topic that I read
all the science fiction books the library had, and read new ones as
fast as the books were put on the shelves. I didn't think that space
travel would really happen in my lifetime because rocket speeds that
I read about were not great enough to overcome earth's gravity and
go far out into space. I dreamed about being a space-traveler, but
didn't know the word astronaut or realize that I would live to see a
very distant-cousin of mine, Neil Armstrong, be the first man to set
foot on the moon.

I was interested in making rockets, and in the chemistry of rocket
fuels. In the field next to our back yard was an old deep gully with
big limestone boulders in it. It became our rocket testing grounds.

Neighbors Norman, David, Doug and sometimes John Mark Wyse, who lived further up the hill, were my accomplices. I was the mad chemist and rocket designer. I could make gunpowder, but I wanted to have a slower-burning fuel. So I experimented with cooking some of my own chemical brews. Yes, I cooked fuel mixtures dissolved in water on our old wood and coal-burning kitchen range. I don't know that Momma or any of the adults or older siblings actually knew what I was doing, and I won't reveal my secrets because I don't want to be sued for someone's experiment gone wrong. So don't try this at home. When I became a college student I worked at night in a hospital and was often called to the emergency room to help with accident patients. One night, a boy came in who was trying to make a rocket. He had blown off part of his hands. This is serious business and does take a great deal of caution in order to stay safe.

I am thankful that I never hurt myself or anyone else by my rocket experiments. I did succeed in making a rocket fuel in solid form from my brews on the stove, but it took quite some time to dry it away from the stove, because I didn't want it to burn up our kitchen. It never did burn except for when I deliberately set it on fire and in a safe place. My fuse invention helped greatly in keeping us safe and away from the explosions. I used a button from an old electric doorbell to ignite my fuses with a strong electric shock. The fuses exploded blue-white hot like the magnesium in my chemistry set, but it was not made of magnesium. My solid fuel worked very well to ignite our rockets at a countdown to zero and blast off. Some of the rockets did explode, but we were always protected by a strong safety barrier, which we usually built of large rocks in our gully rocket-testing base. At least one of our rockets climbed some distance into the air before it fizzled and fell back down to the ground.

My rockets were all quite small, and didn't even match many 4th of July rockets. I had fun and did learn a lot, but I never became a rocket scientist or astronaut. I did, however, become a chemistry teacher in college, and my friend, Norman Shank, also became a chemistry professor. So perhaps something worthwhile came out of my rocket experiments in addition to the fun and frustration that we experienced.

CHAPTER 34: *Learning a More Difficult Lesson*

*O*nce I was in high school, I spent less time at home. Some of my older siblings had already left home to begin their adult lives. When I was at home in the evenings, I spent more time with Momma. We didn't always get along well together. Momma had had several small strokes, something which I didn't really understand. She seemed to worry and to complain a lot. I was ashamed of her at times. She had been an active woman, and I believe that she was quite intelligent and thoughtful in her younger years, but now as she was approaching sixty, she was having real physical and mental difficulties. Sometimes we argued. In these respects I was a normal teenager beginning to think and act independently.

One evening after we had eaten we were standing around talking, probably arguing. Suddenly, her words became slurred and she didn't seem to be able to walk normally. I helped her to lie down on the sofa in the next room, but I thought she was play-acting to get some sympathy. However, she did not improve. Poppa knew that it was serious, and somehow we got her to the car and took her to the hospital. The doctor said that she had had a very bad stroke. They kept Momma in the hospital. By now I was feeling very badly.

My teachers were kind and helpful, which helped me to feel better. They took this as an opportunity to talk about what happens when you have a stroke, and how the damage caused to the brain affects many actions of the patient. If brain damage was on the right side of the brain there might be the effect of paralysis on the left side of the body. Momma was partially paralyzed and that was why I had had to help her get to the sofa to lie down. Strokes could affect how a person felt and acted. This explained some of Momma's behavior about which I had felt ashamed.

Momma's condition did not improve in the hospital. The doctor thought that she might die. The doctor said that she had a strong heart, and that was what kept her alive. One day, all of the members of our family who could, were gathered around her hospital bed. She was breathing heavily, could not talk and could not move normally. She didn't even seem to know that we were in the room with her. At one point, she took a very deep breath and then was completely silent and still. We knew that she was gone. We just stood there dumbfounded for a while. I believe that after a while, the nurses and the doctor came into the room. There was nothing more that we could do, except to go home.

I was experiencing terribly mixed-up emotions. I was sad and crying inside. A part of me was relieved, and another part of me felt regrets. I was now a motherless child, even though my older sisters had been like mothers to me in some ways. In addition, our close neighbors, Arminta Shank, Grace Suter and Grace Hostetter, who were my friends' mothers, often treated me like a part of their own families, and acted like mothers to me.

Momma's funeral was held at Lindale Mennonite Church where I had been baptized. Pastor and EMC President J. R. Mumaw preached the sermon. There is much I do not remember. My emotions were still churning inside me. Mother had chosen her own funeral text. She was expecting her death. The text was from the bible story of Mary who had anointed Jesus' head and feet with an expensive perfume. Some of the disciples were upset because they thought that she had wasted a whole year's worth of wages. Instead, Jesus commended her for preparing him for his burial. He said that, "she had done what she could." These were the words of the bible text, and they summed up Mother's life.

This experience was a very difficult lesson for me to learn. I still wrestle with it sometimes. It is part of the great drama of the meaning of life and death. I have accepted that in her later years, Mother was not always responsible for what she said or did. In her heart and in my heart, I know that she loved us and wanted only the best for us. I know that sometimes she was even proud of me.

Hercules beetle above, Rinosceros beetle below.

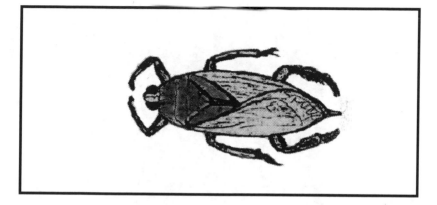

Giant Waterbug and Kestrel hovering

SECTION 4: LATER TEENS

CHAPTER 35: *Flight of the Kestrels*

One gorgeous Saturday morning in summertime, I was hiking several miles across the fields to my friend David Mumaw's farm. The sky was a clear blue with puffy cumulus clouds. The air was warm but not hot. The meadow grasses of the pasture were starting to turn yellow and dry, but underneath were plenty of fresh green new blades of grass. Along the fencerow were trees, one with a hole that would be a good place for Flickers, Blue Birds or Kestrels to nest. I sat down in the grass to rest and watch.

Soon I spotted a pair of Kestrels, a male and a female, like my Killy Killy and Rufus Red-tail. They were perched near the tree that had the hole in it, which I thought could be their nest tree. They were watching the meadow grass, probably looking for mice or grasshoppers. I just sat still and quietly waited to see what would happen. Suddenly the female took off, but she did not dive to the ground to catch something or hover, as Kestrels sometimes do looking for game. She flew upward and soon caught a summer updraft. She no longer beat her wings, but fanned her tail looking much like a miniature Redtailed Hawk soaring on a thermal updraft. Soon her mate joined her.

I lay down in the grass and just enjoyed watching them. The grass felt soft and cool under me. It was a good time to relax and enjoy the day, or even to daydream. The Kestrel pair circled higher and higher. Soon I could no longer tell what kind of birds they were; they were only black specks spiraling higher and higher. I strained to continue to see their tiny dots, but then they disappeared from sight. I kept lying still in the cool grass and pondering the wonder of what I had experienced. I would have enjoyed soaring in the air, simply for fun. Is that what the kestrels had done? Was this some kind of aerial mating dance? Falcons have wonderful vision, but I doubt that they had been hunting small creatures in the meadow below. Perhaps they would have been able to swoop down to catch some hapless small bird flying beneath them. Was it fun and games? Or was it serious life-sustaining falcon survival work? I may never know, but for me it was a time to enjoy and ponder the wonder of creation.

I have always loved airplanes, ever since I was a boy. I had a book about the development of aviation. I knew Leonardo Da Vinci's drawings of bird flight and flying machines. I had seen pictures of early gliders used before powered flight. I thought about and sometimes drew my own pictures of gliders that I wished I could build, but somehow never did. I thought of taking flying lessons, but never felt that I could afford them. I did, however, as a grown man often fly on business, all around our great and wonderful country, including Alaska. I saw and experienced many things that my little Kestrel friends could never have known. I still think that it would be wonderful to fly free as they seemed to fly, without noise or the restriction of an airplane window. I have been struck by lightning while flying in a plane, have seen smoke coming out of the cockpit, and have circled for an hour or so with a sparking jet engine, but I always landed safely, followed by a number of fire trucks. I'm glad my falcon friends don't have such experiences. There is still something wonderfully special about bird flight that only a bird may know, which is not even matched by the exhilaration of hang-gliding. I still am in awe of birds.

CHAPTER 36: *The Last Peregrine Falcons*

$\mathcal{B}$oth David and I were quite excited about what we had read about falconry, and wanted to work with a larger falcon than a Kestrel. Peregrine Falcons were about the size of a crow and had often been used for this sport. They were even called Duck Hawks, but officially should be called Peregrine Falcons. They nest on rocky mountain ledges. We wondered if we could find any Peregrines in the wild, wonderful parts of our Shenandoah Valley. A ridge of mountains called the Massanutten stretches along the central part of the Shenandoah Valley for about 50 miles, from Harrisonburg to Strasburg. Farther east are the Blue Ridge Mountains with the well-known Shenandoah National Park, and still farther west are the Allegheny Mountains. We were blessed with many rocky mountain ledges to search where Peregrine Falcons could nest.

We had sometimes climbed the Massanutten Peak not too far from where we lived, but had never seen falcons there. Perhaps it was too popular a spot for human climbers, and the Peregrines found wilder lodging elsewhere. About twenty-five miles north from our home was Mount Jackson. During the Civil War, General Stone Wall Jackson baffled the Union troops by appearing and disappearing at Mount Jackson in unexpected ways. In this area the Massanutten Ridge divides into two ridges. Between the ridges is the Hidden Valley where Jackson hid his troops. Quite visible from Rt. 11 or Interstate 81 is the significant south-facing cliff of Massanutten Sandstone. This seemed to be an ideal place for us to explore.

David prepared by getting and making ropes to rappel down with from the top of the cliff to look for ledges where falcons might nest. He interested his father, Homer, not only in taking us there in the family car, but also in joining us in our search. It seemed like a long time to wait, but finally the much-anticipated day arrived. We took along packed lunches and started on our search by mid-morning. The first task was to climb the mountain behind the cliff. The going was fairly easy at first. It was only a short hike from the roadside where we parked into the forest that ran up to the top of the mountain. We had to pick our way carefully because there was no well-worn path as there was for climbing the Massanutten Peak. This was a good sign because it likely meant no humans were disturbing potential nesting sites on the cliff. Soon the climb got more difficult, but we continued scrambling upward through the rocks and brush. It was past noon, and we were hungry, when we reached the top. We worked our way over to the rocky ledge at the edge of the cliff, and sat down to eat our lunch.

Turkey Vultures were circling about in the mountain updrafts. Some flew very near over our heads and then went out over the valley almost at our eye level. Suddenly we saw a crow-sized bird turn and then make a steep stoop as it dived to chase away a vulture. It was a Peregrine Falcon! We were delighted. Perhaps this falcon was trying to protect its nesting area. Falcon eggs might be quite tasty to a vulture. The intruding vulture soon knew that it had met its match. It turned out over the valley and away from the cliff. The Peregrine disappeared as quickly as it had appeared, somewhere into the blue sky. Now we had another challenge. Was this falcon really nesting, and could we find the nest?

David's father searched to the north and east, while David and I looked along the rocky ledges around the top of the main cliff near where we had first seen the falcon. We did not see the falcon again, but felt its presence somewhere above us. Would it attack us directly like the Blue Jays had in my back yard? A falcon swooping down at 150 miles per hour or more can deliver a fatal blow that might break the neck of a duck or even a goose. I did not relish the idea of what it might do to me. On the other hand, I believed that these falcons were shy birds, and might avoid humans. I remembered how shy I had been as a boy that I ran to hide behind a door when relatives from Pennsylvania came to visit our family in Virginia. A shy falcon was nothing to fear. Surprisingly, we stumbled across a nest on a broad rock ledge that was quite accessible. There were two cream-colored eggs with rust-brown markings, almost the size of a hens egg. The nest was just a hollowed-out area among the loose pebble-sized rocks on the ledge. This was certainly the nest of the kingly Peregrine Falcon.

David's father soon returned. He was a great naturalist and experienced birder. He had found two interesting nests. One nest belonged to a Raven, the other to a Black Vulture that already had hatchlings. Mr. Mumaw agreed that the nest we had found was that of a Peregrine Falcon. What a day we had had already!

We knew that we could easily find our way back to the falcon nest, so we went to look at the young Black Vultures. Unlike the white down of the young Turkey Vulture that we had unsuccessfully tried to raise, these babies were covered with peach-colored down. We did not disturb them. We had learned our lesson about trying to raise vultures and were glad to leave them alone. I did not see the Raven's nest as it was further away, but Mr. Mumaw did identify a Raven that flew nearby. It was the first that I had seen a Raven for sure. I could add it to my life-long list of birds. It was larger and had a much heavier beak than an ordinary crow. Its call was a rough croak, not a caw-caw like that of a crow.

We were soon planning our return trip to find baby Peregrine Falcons in their nest, but for now we were ready to head for home after a memorable day. We would have to wait several weeks for the falcons to complete their clutch of eggs, incubate and hatch them. Finally, at school one day, David said that his father was ready to take us back to check on the falcon's nest on the following Saturday.

We found our previous parking spot and started our scramble up the mountain. Finally, all hot and sticky, we came out on the top. Anxiously we made our way toward the nest. After some initial wrong turns, we finally came to the hollowed-out spot where the nest was. To our great disappointment, all we found were some broken eggshells. We did not see any baby or adult falcons. What could have happened? We could conjure up all kinds of disaster tales, but we really didn't know. At the time it was a mystery. We did not see the falcons again.

Years later we were able to piece together what was likely the sad tale of what had happened. We may have seen the last nesting pair of Peregrine Falcons in the Shenandoah Valley. Many hawks, eagles and falcons were disappearing across the country, and even pest-eating songbirds were disappearing. Rachel Carson wrote her well-known book, "Silent Spring" to warn of the imminent danger of losing many of our birds. The birds' silent killers were pesticides, particularly DDT. In the case of our falcons, DDT would have caused their eggs to have defective shells. These eggs were so fragile that even the mother's weight while incubating could crush them. We had found the tragic results of pesticides, with only broken eggshells left in the nest.

I do not want to stop this story with this tragic ending. Good things have happened since insecticides like DDT have been banned. Once on a working trip to Denver, Colorado, I came across a group of birders with binoculars and spotting scopes looking up at the ledge of a tall office building. One of the birders invited me to take a look through his scope. There I saw a Peregrine Falcon sitting on its nest. Falcons have been successfully introduced into a number of large cities where there is often an abundance of unwanted pigeons and starlings for the falcons to eat. In recent years, Shenandoah Valley has had nesting falcons again. We did not see the last of the Peregrine falcons after all. The falcons have returned!

CHAPTER 37: *Shells in the Fire, Run!*

$\mathcal{A}$ number of my friends had 22-caliber rifles. They are not usually used for hunting rabbits unless you are a very good and quick shooter. Fall was rabbit-hunting season, and a group of us sometimes got together to hunt. I used Poppa's old Stevens twenty-two for hunting. It was a short light, single shot. It didn't have the accuracy for distance shots that a longer-barreled gun would have. It also had to be reloaded after every shot, so if you missed the first shot you likely didn't get a second shot at an animal or bird. Those are my excuses for not being too successful as a hunter with Poppa's little rifle. Some of the fellows had bolt-action rifles, and some of them would get a second shot. Lefty had a double-barreled shotgun that "broke" open to put in new shells, but he could take two shots before reloading. Despite my lack of success, I had some fun hunting and could tell stories of the one that I missed, a little like those tall fishermen's tales.

One Saturday a group of us got together on the Mumaw farm, Russell, David, Lefty Yoder, David Wenger and I. We combed the fields of the farm by forming a side-by-side line as we walked. Soon we had scared up a rabbit. Someone shouted, "There it goes!" We all raised our guns and fired as quickly as we could. Bang, bang, bang, bang, bang our guns went. Dust kicked up around the fleeing rabbit, but--it got away. We knew that other rabbits would likely just sit tight until one of us almost stumbled over them after all the noise that we had made. With our walking line we would likely dislodge any sitting rabbit at very short range.

We kept marching along. Soon a frightened bunny jumped up almost under my feet. "There she goes," I yelled. There was another series of bangs. I believe that mine came in last – I was too excited. There were some puffs of dust, but then the rabbit keeled over. It had been hit by several sharpshooters. Russ thought that he got in a hit, and so did David Wenger. I was quite sure that I had missed with my late shot. Russ collected our first small game. We continued hunting for quite a while, but only had one more successful event.

We were getting cold and hungry. Someone suggested that we stop to eat our lunches, and build a fire to keep warm. The Mumaws had a little woodlot with a small clearing where we could take shelter. Russ and David had made a ring of rocks in the clearing for campfires. There were some sticks to be burned, and soon we had a cheery blaze going. We all stood around the fire to get warm. We made sure that our guns would not go off accidentally. Lefty broke open his shotgun so that it couldn't shoot, and hung it over his shoulder.

We were getting warmed up and having fun talking about our hunting adventures. While leaning toward the warmth of the fire, Lefty accidentally tipped the barrels of his shotgun forward, and his shells fell out of the double barrels into the fire. Russ saw it happening, and he yelled, "Shells in the fire, run!" We all scattered like scared rabbits. We weren't sure what might happen, but we knew that we didn't want to be close to the fire if the shells exploded and sprayed shot at us. Then we heard a puff, puff, and knew that the danger had passed. Apparently the shell casing had burned through before the shells could detonate, and the gunpowder had simply burned off with a little puff. We were all safe and thankful. Now we had another hunting tale to tell.

Chapter 38: *What We Found in an Old Cedar Tree*

𝒥t was Saturday morning--no school. I needed something different other than housebound activity. Motors could wait. All the odds and ends piled on the table in my room, what was my junk to Mother, but to me were my treasures for my next electrical experiment could wait. I was restless. Mother would have called it cabin fever. Even the *Book of Knowledge* in my brother's room didn't entice me that morning. I wasn't even up for a game of chess, not that I could have found someone to play with me. Winning, which I likely would do, wasn't the game for me that day.

I looked out of my upstairs bedroom window. The sun was shining for once. It looked like it would be a clear, crisp day with a hint of early spring. My sluggish, dull winter spirit stirred. It was time for a good hike. Winter hadn't brought the excitement of a good snow. Winter likely was over – unless we got a March surprise of several feet of snow as we sometimes did in the Shenandoah Valley. But now it was late February and I was ready for spring and new outdoor adventures.

I hurriedly pulled on my coat and cap, and called to Mother that I was going out for a hike, and would be back in time for lunch. She called back "OK, but take care." I felt annoyed that she was always worrying about me. Well this time I wasn't headed for a cave that I had to skinny through a tight hole in which I might get stuck, so I called back, "Don't worry, Mother", and I hurried out the door.

I went over to Norman's house. Norman was also eager for a hike. I suggested that we go to the fields to the north, and see what creatures might be stirring about this fine day. Maybe a groundhog would be out looking for his shadow. If we could scare him back in, perhaps we could keep him from thinking that winter would continue for another 6 weeks. We ducked through a hole in the fence. It was fortunate that there were no cattle in the field, since the old rusty fence wasn't really much of a barrier.

We climbed the hill past the gullies that seemed to be like canyons when I was younger and explored them. They were no adventure for today. A few hardy plants were poking their heads out through the dry pasture grass. The crisp air was invigorating and the warm sun inviting. It was just plain fun to walk in the fields in the fresh air. My restlessness was gone, and my senses were tuned to adventures that lay ahead.

A few vultures were circling above on lazy wings, riding the updrafts. I felt envious. I would like so much to fly like that. I had often dreamed of building a glider to do it. But I knew enough from reading about the Wright Brothers that I had no confidence I would succeed in flying, even if I did try to build a glider. "Hey", Norman said, "look at the crows over on the next hill. I wonder if we could find a crow's nest. You know, a crow could make a great pet. I heard that if you split its tongue, it can learn to talk like a parrot." I didn't know that splitting a crow's tongue would help it to talk, but looking for a nest sounded like fun. We continued our hike to the next hill with our eyes and ears open, but keeping our mouths shut.

Hills in Rockingham County were typically rocky. This hill had lots of thistles in the summer that attracted butterflies. Another thing that always intrigued me was the cannon-ball-sized rocks piled under the cedar trees on top of the hill. I headed in their direction. I really wanted to dig out the rocks sometime and find what might be under that pile of rocks. Maybe the rock piles were Indian graves, or perhaps they were hiding some civil war trophy. One of our buddies, George, had even found an old bayonet in a trash dump near our house. Anyway, the cedar trees were a good place in which to look for a crow's nest.

Sure enough, as we came closer, we scared a crow out of one of the cedars. There it was, a rough nest built of sticks. Would we be lucky and find some eggs or even baby crows? We hiked over to the tree. The first branch on the tree was fairly high up. I started to shinny up the tree like a bear cub, and was able to reach the branch. Once I pulled myself up to that first branch the rest of the climb was easy. I cautiously raised my face to look over the edge of the rather large nest. I also kept an eye out lest the mother crow returned. I didn't want to be dive-bombed and pecked at like we were when we climbed the tree in our backyard to the Blue Jay's nest. I could imagine that a crow's peck would be a serious affair.

I got my first glance over the brim of the nest. I saw three speckled grayish-white downy balls that looked like newly-hatched baby chicks. One of them lifted its head and opened its beak wide to be fed. It was indeed a baby crow and its two brothers or sisters. Unfortunately I had no food for it. Its eyes barely seemed to open. It must have just hatched. It seemed unafraid. I felt bonded to it, and perhaps it bonded to me, and thought that I was its mother. I called down to Norman, and told him what I had found and soon I scrambled down the tree. It was Norman's turn. He was shorter than I was, so I gave him a push to get up to the first branch and he got to look into the nest.

When we both were back on the ground, we began to plot how we could have pet crows. We knew that they were too little to take out of the nest for the time being, but we could wait. We would have to convince our parents to let us keep crow nestlings, and we would need to find a place to keep them and learn how to feed them. We were both excited as we hurried home. We were also a little afraid that we might not be able to get them at just the right time. Would something bad happen to them before we could take them out of the nest?

CHAPTER 39: *Will We Get Pet Crows?*

$\mathcal{I}$t was several weeks before we got back to the nest again. In the meantime, I had read all I could find about keeping a crow as a pet. I learned that it could eat just about anything that a human would eat. But as a growing baby, it needed a good protein diet to grow strong enough to fly and have glossy black, well-formed feathers. That was no problem. We were a big family with lots of table scraps. In the summer we had a big garden with lots of wholesome vegetables and tomatoes. But better yet, Poppa worked for the largest poultry hatchery east of the Mississippi. We could get an ample supply of eggs and even little chicks that would make excellent food for our baby crow. It would be my job to keep the ever-hungry young bird well-fed, but that would be a challenge and fun.

I discussed everything with my best friend, David Mumaw. He, too, was excited about raising a pet crow. Living on a farm he had more opportunities for animal adventures than I did. He even had found a nestling crow himself. His was a most unusual bird because it was not black. David's dad was a biology teacher, and he kept his eye out for unusual things in nature. They once had a partially albino barn swallow that had a little dark blue coloring, but was largely white. It stayed around on the farm for several summers, but finally disappeared. David's crow was not the normal white albino with pink eyes. It was coffee-colored, sort of like coffee with a lot of cream added. It also had dark eyes. It was probably an outcast to the other crows.

Well, finally one Saturday Norman and I were both able to get away and go to check on the crow's nest we had found. We hiked the hills as quickly as we could. This time, Norman was the first to climb up to the nest. He sounded excited. "They're here, John," he called down. After he came down, I took my turn scrambling up the tree. There were three hungry babies extending their necks and opening their mouths to be fed. In fact, they were chirping or cawing as though their lives depended on it. Come to think of it, their lives did depend on it. Fortunately for us, their mother was absent just then. I immediately saw that they were still too small to take home with us. I had found before that it was best to wait until bird babies were mostly feathered and almost ready to fly when they were taken from the nest. Waiting until they were ready also cut down on the time we would have to spend in the feeding clamoring babies stage. They would still bond with us as though we were their mothers, if ours was the hand that fed them.

I told Norman the bad news. We would have to wait a week or two longer. It would give us more time to prepare for them. We had both found places our parents would let us keep baby crows. Mine was in the little chicken house since we weren't using it for chickens anymore. Another place I could keep a baby crow was under our side porch since that space was enclosed by lattice and had a door.

Since we had gotten to the nest early in our day, we had plenty of time for another adventure. There was that rock pile that I thought could be an Indian cairn. This might be a good day to excavate it. In my grade school Virginia history class, I had learned that

Indians had lived in the Shenandoah Valley long before white people had come to the Valley. I also knew that people sometimes found arrowheads in newly-plowed fields. Once David Messner and I were walking along the top of the hill near where he lived when he spied a large arrow or spearhead lying on the bare ground. He had given it to me for my rock collection. I added the spearhead to my wampum hammer or whatever it was that someone had found on the Shenandoah Mountain. So I was eager to make my own archaeological find. I called back to Norman, who was still under the crow's nest tree. "Would you help me dig out a hole here at the bottom of this pile of rocks? It might be an Indian grave. We might make a real haul." Norman was willing – he often went along with my proposed adventures, and he had some of his own, that I helped him to do.

We started throwing out rocks to make a hole about two feet wide. We soon got warm enough with all of this work that we had to take off our jackets. After what seemed to be a long time we were down only two feet. It was a lot of work. In my mind, I could almost picture a dozen Indian warriors, throwing rocks onto the pile to make a sacred heap over their departed chief. Well, we would have a lot more work to do to equal a dozen Indian warriors. I was still game to work to reach the bottom, even if it took until noon. And that is about how long it took. Sadly, we found no bones, no arrow or spearheads, no peace pipes, or anything that looked like a human artifact. We just found rocky valley soil at the bottom of our hole. My worst scenario was likely true. Some farmer had dumped a wagonload of stones gathered from his fields into what might have been a depression left from a sinkhole in our limestone soil. We were not successful archaeologists, after all. After a disappointing morning, with two disappointments under our belts, we slowly slunk homeward. But not all hope was lost. There were still growing crows in the nest, and I had finally put my inquisitive mind to rest about this pile of rocks.

It was another week or two until we were again hurrying to the crow's nest. When we got there we saw a mostly fledged crow chick sitting on the edge of the nest. Every once in a wile it would flap its wings as if it were about to fly, but it didn't get anywhere. It was my turn to climb the tree. Up, up I went. I could see that the babies were getting nervous, but they were still not able to fly. They still had some grayish down sticking out from under their feathers. It seemed like just the right time to take two of them for our pets. Luckily, their tired parents were once again out scavenging for food for the hungry chicks. I called down to Norman. "How shall I get them down? I can't carry them and climb down. How about if I just drop them to you one at a time? Their wings are big enough that they likely won't be hurt." "OK," Norman replied, "I'm ready."

I reached over to the biggest baby sitting on the edge of the nest. It moved away a little, but it wasn't so afraid that I couldn't catch it in my hand. It protested, but I held it out where there was a clear drop to the ground. It fluttered its wings on the way down, but landed softly not too far from Norman. He soon had it in the bottom of the burlap bag which we had brought along to carry them home in. Then I dropped a second one. It too landed safely, and Norman tucked it in beside its nest mate. We had pet crows at last!

CHAPTER 40: *Jimmy Hitches a Ride*

℘or the next several months Norman and I became very busy surrogate-parents in addition to being school students, but I don't think that our grades suffered. We were excited and committed to being successful. I called my crow Jimmy and Norman called his Blackie. We never did know their sex, but we both thought of them as boys. They were demanding children, and seemed to immediately accept us as their parents. They had seen us at a very young age when we visited their nest. I think that they bonded to us. That is the term biologists use. Our pet crows looked forward to our coming to feed them, and soon they were following us around, even before they could fly.

I gave Jimmy a rich diet of milk or egg-soaked bread crusts, and quite a variety of table scraps. He was growing fast and was often doing trial wing flaps that began to lift him off the ground, or from the perch I had made for him in our little chicken house. One day when I came in, he flew right off the perch and surprised both of us by landing right on my shoulder. This soon became his favorite spot for him to perch. His first flight was a little clumsy, but it was remarkable how fast his flying skills improved. Soon, he was flying wherever he wanted to inside the chicken house. Jimmy's feathers were a sleek and shiny black, and I was sure that he was healthy. He made all kinds of crow noises, including many noises I had never heard a wild crow make. I never detected words, but to Poppa the calls sounded enough like children that sometimes he mistakenly thought there were children playing, when it was only Jimmy carrying on like a much-excited child.

The real test of our bond was still to come, for I had never let Jimmy fly freely outdoors. One nice spring day, Mother was hanging up wash on the wash-line at the side of our house. I thought this would be a good day to let Jimmy fly free. I walked out of the little chicken house with Jimmy perched on my shoulder. He spied a white handkerchief waving on the wash line. He flew off my shoulder in a flash and landed on the line next to the handkerchief. One quick peck, and Jimmy had jerked away the clothespin holding the hanky. Then he caught the white cloth by a corner and sailed right up to the top of roof of our house. Jimmy's white flag blew proudly in the light breeze. But this was not a flag of surrender. It was Jimmy's public announcement that "I am the king of the mountain!" Well, at least he was king of the house roof, and I would not be able to get him down from there unless he decided to come down himself. I went inside and got a crust of bread and soaked it in milk. This was one of Jimmy's favorite foods. When I walked outside and looked up, Jimmy was still perched on the ridge of the house roof with his handkerchief flag. He looked down at me and the bread crust for a minute or two. Then he let the handkerchief blow out of his beak, and it slowly drifted to the ground. The flag game was over. There was a more important matter for this young, ever-hungry crow. Jimmy swooped down to my shoulder and pecked the bread right out of my raised fingers. He stayed right there on my shoulder as I walked back into the chicken house to give him the rest of his morning meal. From then on, we were buddies, indoors or out. If he flew off my shoulder to check out something that had caught his crow eye, he was soon flying back to me as I walked away.

One of my prized possessions at this time was a bright red bicycle I used to ride to school and around our little town of Park View. My older brothers had their own bikes long before me, the "baby of the family," as Mother still sometimes called me, to my chagrin. You see, bicycles cost a lot of money for a large poor family struggling to make ends meet on Poppa's small earnings at the hatchery. We had to pay for many of the things we wanted with our own money, after helping to pay for our own tuition at the local Christian school. I worked raising chickens at home to earn my way, but my older brothers soon found better jobs, and were able to get their own bicycles. When one of them got a newer, bigger bike, they took pity on their little brother. Was it my ceaseless begging to be allowed to ride their bikes that gave them the idea for getting me one just to get me off their backs? Or, could it just have been my insistent begging for my own bike that spurred their generosity? In any case, they worked together and fixed up the old bicycle, and painted it bright red just for me. I was certainly proud of it, and it gave me quick wheels for going wherever I wanted in town.

So what do you think Jimmy did when his master rode off quickly on the bicycle? Well, Jimmy could fly faster than I could ride, so he had no trouble staying right with me. He could easily land on my shoulder whenever he wanted. At some time, he even learned the trick of flying just ahead of me. One day, he surprised me by fluttering just in front of my face, then landing directly on the handlebar of the bicycle. After that, he was like a dog that likes to stick his head out an open window while riding in a car. Jimmy's favorite place was right on the handlebar when I was riding my bicycle and he was loose outside. He flew off and came back whenever he desired. So we became biking companions.

From that time on, I never feared that Jimmy would leave me. He somehow found his place in our human family, and he didn't seem to notice that he was a crow. There were plenty of wild crows in the fields next to our house, but Jimmy never seemed to give them a second's notice. We were his crow clan, and that was that.

CHAPTER 41: *Jimmy and the Red Hat*

$\mathcal{S}$ome creatures are colorblind, but not most birds, and definitely not crows. Crows can be hoarders of little objects that catch their eye. It could be a brightly colored pebble, or a shiny piece of metal. Jimmy gathered things, but I never found where he hid them. I might see him with something, but then it was gone.

Red was a color that excited Jimmy. He liked my red bicycle, and the rides that he took with me. This is a little gory, but he also liked bloody, red meat. It was food to him. You see, we were an ex-farm family. I don't remember our farm. We moved away from the farm when I was only about two years old. But you can't take farm habits out of a family. We had a big garden, much to Jimmy's delight. He liked tomatoes, but perhaps you'll remember that I, for the most part, except for the little round cherry tomatoes, disliked tomatoes. We raised a lamb, we had chickens, as did some of our neighbors, and once Poppa even raised pigs, which was against the stipulations on our property deed. When a neighbor complained about the pigs' smell, the hogs had to go. We went to a farmer friend for butchering. Raw, bloody, red meat scraps were devoured by Jimmy with relish.

We butchered some of our chickens. I learned to stretch a chicken's neck between two nails on the chopping block and to whack off its head with an ax. Thinking about this today almost turns my stomach, but it was just the way we lived then. The chicken would flop free from the block, even with its head cut off. There would be a minute of wild flopping, sometimes with red blood spurting out of the severed neck. So did you ever hear the expression: "Flopping around like a chicken with its head cut off?" Jimmy never seemed to mind this execution of a relative, if there was in it his share of bloody tidbits. But those came only after the chicken was soaked in hot water and all the feathers had been plucked off. We would take a burning tube of paper to singe the remaining little quills popping out of the chicken's skin. Finally the chicken was gutted and cut up, and that's when Jimmy got his share.

So now you might see why Jimmy was particularly excited when he saw the color red. Once a little boy came to visit, and of course, we showed him Jimmy the crow. Unfortunately the boy was wearing a red baseball hat. Jimmy immediately spied the red hat. He flew directly at the boy, and landed right on his head. Jimmy began to wildly peck at the red hat, and the boy began to cry. I'm sure it was more than just the fright he got of a crow flying directly at him. Jimmy was a full-grown crow, and his beak was sharp and strong. He could easily tear pieces off a chunk of red meat and eat them. Those crow pecks must have really hurt the little boy's head, even through his cap. I had to grab Jimmy by his legs the way I had learned to catch chickens and take him directly to his chicken house room. In the meantime, others comforted the little boy. Both he and Jimmy had had a bad day. From then on, I carefully watched to make sure that Jimmy didn't fly after red hats, but as far as I know, it never happened again.

Chapter 42: *Jimmy Goes to School*

$\mathscr{P}$ark School, where most of us Stahl children went to grade school, was just across the field from where we lived, as you may remember. Only our oldest brother, Omar, didn't attend there because he had started at Eastern Mennonite School, EMS, just two blocks south of our house. When my siblings completed seventh grade at Park School, they immediately went to EMS as high school freshmen. Virginia didn't have an 8th grade until right after my sister Sara, who was four years older than I, completed grade school. The state was still experimenting with what and where 8th grade should be. For me it turned out to be at EMS. So like the others, I graduated from Park School upon completing 7th grade.

However, it wasn't long until I was going to Park School every morning or evening and even some Saturdays. You see, Wilbur Pence, the Superintendent of Rockingham County Schools, gave me a job as school janitor by the time I was a high school freshman.

Well, really, I kind of inherited the job from my brother Jacob, who was my next-oldest brother. I used to go and help Jacob sometimes in cleaning or at least watching what he did. The floors were black, oiled wood floors, kind of yucky, even after Jacob had swept them as well as he could. In the winter, he also had to start the fires in the big coal stoves, one in each of the three classrooms. I also remember joining in when my brother had to dig paths for the students through almost two feet of snow. He cleared the front walk and the back path to the outhouses. There was no indoor plumbing, except for a drinking fountain in the hallway.

Being the "spoiled" one, I had a lot better job than Jacob had had. The school made an addition to the back of the building with in-door restrooms, and a coal-fired furnace in the basement. They also refurbished the classrooms. I only needed to sweep nice light-colored, waxed floors, and stir up the furnace fire and get it going well before the teachers and students arrived. Sometimes I was in too much of a hurry, which once almost led to disaster, but that's another story for another time. The point of this story is that Jimmy the crow would sometimes follow me to school on Saturdays if I had special work to do. He couldn't go into the building with me, but he would hang out in the giant old oak trees in back of the school, or perch on a railing or swing set until my work was finished. Then he could take his favorite ride home on the bicycle handlebars. So Park School became a favorite hangout for Jimmy. If he wanted to, he could even fly across the field to the school, without the farmer ever seeing him, and anyway, Jimmy never made a path across the winter wheat like me.

I usually kept Jimmy penned up at home while I was at school, so he usually couldn't visit the elementary school students while I was attending my classes. However, one late spring day, Jimmy was out flying about the community around noontime when the days were already quite warm. Park School did not have air conditioning. In the 1950s, when I was growing up, the only people I knew who had air conditioning were wealthy people. So when it got too warm, the teacher would sometimes open the big classroom windows. Jimmy was hanging out at Park School at lunchtime that day. No doubt, activity inside the building caught his attention. For a while he just flew around outside the windows. That caused some excitement among the students who were eating their lunches. Each student had brought his or her own packed lunch from home. After a while, Jimmy's crow brain was sure to tell him that the good times were going on inside the building, and he was missing out on it! So to get his crow share of the good life, he flew in the open window and landed on a student's desk. Perhaps he just wanted a share of the student's lunch. I am sure the little girl sitting in that desk was quite startled, never having had a pet crow with which to share her lunch. Then, too, Jimmy's ethics weren't very well developed; he simply took what he wanted without even saying please. But as a black-feathered member of the human flock he would only take what seemed to him to be his rightful share.

Then Jimmy sighted something more exciting than a sandwich. The little girl had a bright silver spoon with which to eat a part of her lunch. One quick peck, and Jimmy had the spoon in his beak. He knew he had to make his getaway now. Humans had a way of taking things back from him. A quick hop into the air, and Jimmy flew out the window with the spoon. He must have taken it to a favorite hiding place, because it was never found. I wasn't there to see this happening, but the story soon got to me since there were people at school who knew that I had a pet crow. Sadly, something had happened to Norman's Blackie, so that meant that Jimmy was king crow of the neighborhood, and as his owner, I was the young man accountable for any of his misbehavior. Stories and accusations usually had a way of getting back to me. Sometimes I was called to catch Jimmy from a neighbor's yard who didn't particularly appreciate having a crow hanging around their house. But in this case it made an exciting school day for the students. And, if they could only have admitted it, it was an exciting day for the teachers, too. At any rate, all was forgiven, but after that, I did make sure that Jimmy didn't fly around the neighborhood while the students were at Park School.

CHAPTER 43: *Jimmy Visits a Neighbor*

One block toward the college from us and a few houses further up the hill lived Professor Mary Emma Showalter. To us Stahl children, she was the epitome of what it was to be proper. In comparison, we felt a little rough around the edges. We couldn't always understand her. She was one of the few faculty on the staff with a Ph.D. She had written what was the most successful book in our current world of Mennonites. We were secretly proud that our oldest brother, Omar, had typed some of her manuscript while taking college classes at the University of Tennessee where Miss Showalter was completing her doctorate in home economics. She wrote a cookbook as her doctoral thesis. The title was, "The Mennonite Community Cook Book," and copies of it are still being sold decades later, long after its author has passed on to her heavenly realm.

One brother remembers walking to school across a field when it had just begun to rain. He noticed Doctor Showalter driving down the street, so he ran to where her car would pass by, expecting to catch a ride. However, she took no note of him, or perhaps didn't think it proper or necessary to pick up a Stahl boy who was wet and bedraggled. Brother was quite disappointed, and didn't think very kindly of her. He thought that by all means she should have been so courteous as to give a boy, who was trying not to get wet, a ride along to the high school, which was located on the same campus as the college. Most of us children were simply intimidated by Doctor Showalter. I doubt that I would have run to catch a ride with her. Yet I was glad that my brother Omar had no problem working with her. Omar also seemed to live in a higher world than I did.

Jimmy Crow had no such fears or scruples as I did about Miss Mary Emma or her property. This could cause some problems. I also had to take into consideration that Miss A. Grace Wenger, whom I respected even though she was my English teacher, also lived with Miss Mary Emma. I wanted to be on Miss A. Grace's good side, because it seemed that for once I was making good grades in English, and even enjoying it. Jimmy, however, was sometimes attracted to Miss Wenger and Miss Showalter's property. There was a kind of arbor structure in the back yard of their property. Perhaps it had grapes, although I didn't get close enough to find out. Jimmy liked grapes, and he could help himself to those in our own back yard.

One Saturday, Jimmy was out snooping around the neighborhood while I was engaged in other activities. He apparently found something attractive on the Showalter property, so he flew over and landed on the arbor and made himself at home. Pretty soon our phone began to ring. Let me tell you, it was an exciting time when a phone line came to the neighborhood. It was a new electrical device that I knew I had to check out carefully.

The phone was a somewhat fancy wooden box with two bells on the front side near the top. In the middle was a long-necked mouthpiece with a black funnel shape on the end that you could speak into or perhaps shout, if the connection was not very good. On one side of the wooden box was a black receiver with an earpiece that hung on a pronged cradle. When you wanted to listen, you lifted the receiver off the cradle and put the earpiece to your ear. The cradle was lifted up by a spring mechanism, and that made the connection to our party line of eight or so neighbors. It wasn't considered polite to eavesdrop on other people's conversations, but I would guess that most of us children sneaked to the phone and listened sometimes when adults weren't around. At least, to make my own confession, I did. Even adults sometimes inadvertently listened to others' conversations because you had to pick up the receiver to find out if anyone was on the line before you could ring anyone else or the operator. Oh yes, on the other side of the telephone was a crank that you turned to ring up a neighbor. Each neighbor on the line had their own distinctive ring. Ours was three shorts. Some were combinations of shorts and longs. It took some skill to crank out these Morse-code like rings. You could hear everyone's rings, but you were only supposed to answer your own.

The front of the phone was on hinges and opened like a little door. It was the guts inside that intrigued me most. There were two good-sized electric cells that made the battery for powering the phone and sending out messages over the phone line. There also were coils of very fine wire, and interesting switches. If you knew just where to touch, or didn't know but touched these connections accidentally, you could get a good electric shock when you turned the crank. It was a neat trick to play on some unsuspecting victim.

Well, as I already said, that morning when Jimmy was on the loose, our phone rang and Momma answered. Then she called "John, you have got to go over to Mary Emma Showalter's house and get Jimmy. He's causing trouble, and Mary Emma doesn't like it, but she can't chase him away. Now, do it right away. Sometimes I think that crow will be the death of me." I knew by the tone of Momma's voice that I needed to do it right away. So, with some trepidation, I left the house with a treat to attract Jimmy, so I could bring him home and pen him up for the day.

When I got to the Showalter house I saw, to my surprise, both Dr. Showalter and my teacher, Miss A. Grace Wenger, out in the back yard with Jimmy. Mary Emma was trying to chase Jimmy away with a broom. Whenever he landed somewhere, she would run after him waving the broom. Jimmy would fly up just out of her reach, then fly down and perch somewhere else. I almost thought that he was enjoying the game. When I looked at Miss A. Grace, I could see that she was laughing, but I wasn't very happy. I had trouble getting Jimmy's attention.

Now my memory's a little clouded. Perhaps it has blocked out a painful truth. You see, A. Grace Wenger now lives at Landis Homes, a retirement community next to my brother Jacob's farm in Lancaster County, Pennsylvania. We visited my wife Susan's mother there quite often in her older years. Sometimes we would meet A. Grace Wenger there. She reminded me of this incident with my crow. I can tell that she still gets a kick out of it. She told my brother Jacob the story once, and his version doesn't end the way I thought it had ended. I thought that I eventually caught Jimmy when he came for the treat that I had, and then took him home to put him in solitary confinement for the day. Jacob thinks that I couldn't catch Jimmy. I had to go home without him. Then the ladies went into the house to prepare for guests and left Jimmy chattering outside. To dampen the ruckus that Jimmy was making, and so as not to disturb the expected guests, they closed the back window and pulled down the blinds. Jimmy apparently came home in his own good time, but his master was defeated. Which ending would you want for this story? Perhaps you can make one up that you like even better.

There is a short sequel. Miss Mary Emma became Mrs. Ira Eby. She married a widower from Maryland. They built a new house on the top of the hill on the same street. Mary Emma's stepdaughter was Eleanor Eby, who became my high school classmate for our last year or two at EMHS. We also went to college together at EMC, Eastern Mennonite College. After college, Eleanor married my best friend David. Miss Mary Emma no longer intimidated me and I could retell this Jimmy Crow story with some relish in the way that I remembered, or at least the way I thought it should end.

Chapter 44: *Jimmy Goes to Church*

*I*n the spring of 1958, I graduated from high school and was planning to return to Eastern Mennonite College, which was on the same campus as my high school. My brother Jacob was married to Rachel, and they had a young son, Joseph. They lived in Lancaster County, Pennsylvania, in the heart of Mennonite and Amish farm country. I had worked on their farm for part of the previous summer. Jacob badly needed a farm hand, and I needed money for college. I procrastinated writing that I would come to work, being busy with senior activities and caring for Jimmy. Finally, I did get off a short note which Rachel remembers well. It read,

"A quirk will come to work. Don't smirk."

I asked my neighbor and friend Norman to take care of Jimmy and he agreed. He also said that he would write to me. Norman was four years younger than I, but had a bright, inquiring mind. He later became a college chemistry professor, but I had the privilege of becoming one of his college chemistry teachers, because I started teaching some chemistry as a faculty assistant right after I graduated and had a summer of study at Virginia Tech. He was one of my top students. Norman and I played chess by mail that summer. He kept me up-to-date on the neighbor boys' adventures, and on his own summer activities.

A letter dated July 2, 1958 began, "Dear John, I've been working on more theories that might interest you. I have been reading a very interesting book entitled, 'Biography of the Earth.'" Then he elaborated on why the moon is slowly receding from the earth, the book's explanation, and his own ideas about it. After that he got into quantum theory of waves and particles, and Einstein's law of gravity. I'm not sure if I responded to all of Norman's ideas. I was bogged down with feeding and milking Rosy, the cow, early in the morning, picking tomatoes in the hot sun, getting itchy all over from threshing dust and sweat, and harvesting peas until three o'clock in the morning. We had good times too, but it was hard work. I learned that I was not a farmer in many ways, especially as I watched the hay baler chute get caught on the loading wagon as we went around a corner at the end of the field. I was told to watch it. Which I did! But I was supposed to lift it up to ride over the edge of the wagon when we turned a corner. Well, I knew I was ready for more thinking challenges from Norman, and eager to start college in the fall.

Norman was faithfully caring for Jimmy and trying to keep him from getting into too many pranks in the neighborhood. One hot summer Sunday evening as Norman's family was walking to the college chapel which is now Lehman Auditorium, Jimmy was on the loose. Norman's dad, Lester, was to be in charge of the service that evening. Since it was hot and the chapel had no air conditioning in those days, the large windows were wide open. This attracted "bugs" and moths, and other things which could be an interesting diversion for a boy who was a "bug" collector. We didn't have computer bugs in those days, but plenty of the real kind. That evening there was a surprise visitor, one much larger than the largest moth that might fly in the window attracted by the light.

Jimmy the crow had followed Norman's family by stealth. He probably detoured to many interesting spots around the neighborhood along the way. No one had noticed Jimmy as they walked the several blocks to the chapel. Lester took his place in front to lead the service, but Norman sat further back in the audience. As the service was in progress, suddenly a big black bird fluttered through the open window. Soon everyone's attention was on the bird, while Lester was trying to keep the focus on the program. Norman, of course, knew that the bird was Jimmy, and that he had forgotten to pen Jimmy up before they left home. Jimmy settled down quite comfortably on the back of a bench somewhat toward the back of the large auditorium.

Norman got up and walked over to where Jimmy was sitting peacefully enough. He reached out his hand to catch Jimmy. But that evening Jimmy apparently decided that he wanted to be in church with everyone else. Norman's attempts to catch him were futile. Jimmy finally settled on the back of one of the front benches, cocked his head slightly, and seemed to be paying attention to Lester. Lester and the audience finally realized that Jimmy was there to stay. Lester gave some explanation, and the service continued. Norman never did tell me what family conversations followed that incident, and I don't remember how he got Jimmy home. That was Jimmy's only visit to church. He was just being a curious crow. He was a good crow, but before the end of the summer he departed to where all good crows go. I never got to see him again. I have fond memories of my little black-feathered, bonded brother who often followed me like a shadow. I still wish I could fly like Jimmy. If I could swoop around in the air, I might try some tricks of my own.

CHAPTER 45: *Woes and Glory of Latin*

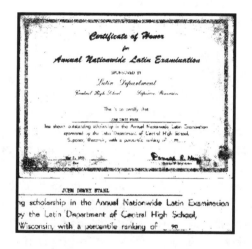

I was now a sophomore in high school. I could choose some elective subjects. My interests were science and math, but I also had learned to like literature, just not grammar. I generally got "As" and "Bs" on my report card. The guidance counselor suggested that I should take Latin, as it would be useful in scientific studies. So I enrolled in Miss Kamrer's Latin One class. Miss Kamrer also taught Latin and Greek in college, and was a very demanding teacher for high school students.

This course involved a lot of memorization, which I did not enjoy. At the beginning of the class, we would all go up to the blackboard to write the lessons we were to have learned. It was only a small class and most of the other students were girls. I always felt embarrassed, and like a fool when I had not done my homework sufficiently well to be able to write the lesson. My many other projects and interests often came before giving my Latin lessons much attention. So I was frequently embarrassed, but not sufficiently penitent to take the time that I needed to study Latin. I got a "C" or a "D" grade in Latin on my first report card, while I got an "A" in every other subject. I piddled along and at least did well enough to get a "C" grade for the semester.

I did eventually learn to conjugate verbs and the declension of nouns to correctly translate or read simple Latin stories or well-known Latin slogans. I knew that "E PLURIBUS UNUM" on coins meant "One out of many," referring to the union of many colonies to form the United States. I also knew that the Virginia state motto "Sic semper tyrannis" meant "thus ever to tyrants," or that unelected kings would be deposed. The Latin did help me later in my college science courses, but it seemed to me like taking bitter medicine. I think that there was only one student who did more poorly than I did in the class, and she soon dropped out, leaving me on the bottom I suppose.

Miss Kamrer gave us a national standardized Latin exam at the end of the course. I feared the worst, and knew that I would not enroll for the next Latin course. I had had my fill of Latin. The dreaded day came when we were to be given our test scores. The first students called were all given certificates for outstanding achievement in Latin. Each had made the 90th percentile or better on the national Latin exam. Then my name was called. I listened with apprehension. Would this be my final shaming in Latin class? I stood up as Miss Kamrer came to my seat. To my great surprise she handed me a certificate, and commended me for achieving 90th percentile nationally in Latin. This was a pleasant ending to my Latin studies, but it was the ending. I did not enroll in Latin Two.

CHAPTER 46: *Code and Kites*

M. T. Brackbill's observatory and planetarium had created an interest in astronomy for my friends and me. Several of us were pursuing a number of interests in addition to astronomy. There were a number of adults in the community who were ham radio operators, and so, many of us developed an interest in radio. We used germanium diodes to make what were called crystal radios. We could listen to several radio stations, particularly at night when the ionosphere reflected radio waves over great distances.

I even tried a somewhat dangerous experiment similar to Ben Franklin's flying a kite in a thunderstorm to improve my radio's reception. I knew something about the power of electrical storms. One evening while we were having a severe thunderstorm, I saw a spark about a foot long jump from the light over our electric range down to the stove burners. During another storm, one of our neighbors, Jacob Esch, had stepped out onto his front porch to see if he could capture a picture of lightning with a little snapshot camera. When the film was developed, he had indeed gotten a picture that looked like our house was being hit by lightning. He gave us a copy of the photo. The lightning was actually far behind our house.

I often flew my kites on the hill or in the open field, below our house, which was no longer used to grow wheat. I had a radio rigged up in an old telephone receiver. I knew that a long, high antenna could help my radio reception. So I took a good kite that I had made, and attached a long "hair-wire" to the tail that was attached to the radio as an antenna. It was a clear summer day with a slight breeze, but no danger of imminent thunderstorms. I didn't want to be electrocuted. Sure enough, the kite lifted about 100 feet of wire almost straight up, and it made an excellent antenna. The trouble was that the breezes were not steady enough to keep my antenna up for very long, but I had done it as an experiment and was not expecting it to be an antenna for long.

I was a pretty good builder, but our neighbor Sam Strong was even better. He had taken a lot of industrial art courses, and had good tools. He had a large, well-made train set with a lot of special features. He also made great kites, like I did. Once he heard about a kite-flying contest nearby in Harrisonburg. There would be prizes for various kinds of kites. So Sam built a box kite with wings that was about as tall as he was. It took very heavy, strong cord to fly it. It had a powerful tug, but thankfully couldn't quite lift us off the ground.

On the day of the kite contest, Sam came to my house to see if I would go with him to the contest. He was sure that he would have the biggest kite. He said there was also a prize for the smallest kite. I thought that would be an easy prize to win. I got two toothpicks, some sewing thread and some very thin tissue paper. Soon I had a little kite, but it flew just fine. So I went with Sam to the contest. We had to walk since Sam's kite couldn't fit into a car. Sure enough, Sam's kite was the biggest, most powerful kite in the contest. No one else had thought of using toothpicks to make a kite, so my kite was the smallest kite that could fly. We walked home with two prizes, just as Sam had thought. Sam went on to get a doctoral degree in industrial arts and taught in the University of Kentucky system. He was chosen to construct the display cases for the first moon rocks that were displayed by the Smithsonian Museum in Washington.

Although I learned Morse code I never became very good at it because I was a poor speller. I never tried to get my ham radio license like some of my friends did. In fact, my friend Russell not only became a ham, but he developed a successful electronics business, as did J. Mark Wyse, who helped with rocket experiments. J. Mark also had an interest in telescopes, and became a friend of a college student and later teacher, John Hershey, who had all kinds of unusual ideas for telescope construction. John eventually became an astronomer and worked for the National Observatory. I soon turned my full interest to telescope construction.

Chapter 47: *Building a Telescope*

*The black pipes and weight are
the polar mounting for tracking.*

$\mathcal{S}$everal of us, Glen and Lowell Kauffman, and George R. Brunk, III started an astronomy and telescope club. It seems that I was chosen to be the club president, but my responsibilities were never well defined. Our first goal was to acquire a telescope that could be used for astronomy. Glen and Lowell found a mail-order place to buy a low cost objective lens for a refractor telescope. They did get the telescope to work, but it was never very satisfactory for astronomy because its image was surrounded with a rainbow of colors, called chromatic aberration, due to the uncorrected objective lens. Large corrected lenses were too expensive for us. The answer to this problem was to build a reflector telescope with a mirror objective such as the one Sir Isaac Newton had invented. This became my goal, but it took me a long time to realize it. Meanwhile I had no planned goals for the astronomy club and it died. George went on to become a successful ham operator, and has had interesting conversations with the King of Jordan, who was also a radio ham. Glenn became a chemistry professor and Lowell became a businessman.

I continued to read books on amateur telescope making, and laying plans to grind a six-inch telescope mirror. It would not be easy, and would take a long time. I saved up my money to buy a six-inch mirror blank and corresponding six-inch tool that would be placed underneath the mirror as it was being ground down. The tool glass becomes convex, thicker in the middle, while the upper mirror becomes concave. Carborundum grit is the medium placed between the two pieces of glass that accomplishes the grinding. The person doing the grinding has to push the mirror blank back and forth while walking around the tool to get the right mirror shape.

I got an old metal 50-gallon drum to hold my tool glass. I poured a layer of concrete several inches thick on top of the barrel with three bolts embedded in the concrete to fasten the glass tool blank. Finally, I was able to buy a mirror kit with a Pyrex mirror blank, a corresponding tool blank and all the sizes of grit and polish that I would need to prepare my mirror. Then I set up my barrel in our basement. I would work at grinding after school and on Saturdays. I had made an aluminum template with the curvature that was needed for the mirror following the pattern in a telescope-making book. It took a long, long time, weeks and months, until the mirror fit the template. I was determined to finish the job. I had once overheard Poppa tell Momma, "John never finishes his projects." Well, I did sometimes, and I would do it again with this project, even if it took me years. Poppa would be wrong this time!

It took over a year, but the day came when an optical test showed the figure cut on the mirror was the correct parabolic shape. I actually had overshot a little, and I detected a slightly hyperbolic shape, but it was so close that it didn't appear necessary to correct it. I sent the mirror off to have it coated with a thin coat of aluminum so that it would reflect as a mirror.

I had to get a metal tube, a small diagonal mirror, and eyepiece lenses. I took an industrial arts course in aluminum casting to make an eyepiece holder that would fit the eight-inch metal furnace pipe that I had acquired for the main telescope tube. I constructed a metal holder for the objective mirror, a "spider" holder for the diagonal mirror that would reflect the mirror's image to the eyepiece on the side of the telescope tube. I made the focal length of the mirror to be 50 inches. That way a one-inch focus eyepiece would result in 50-power magnification, a half-inch focal lens would produce 100-power magnification, and a quarter-inch focal lens would give me a two hundred-power enlargement. I painted the outside of the telescope tube gray, but later changed it to a white plastic cover. The inside was black, so as to not reflect light, which would interfere with the desired image.

It was probably about two years until all the work was finished and I could try out my new telescope. In the daytime I could see starlings sitting on a power line about a mile away. On a clear night I could easily see the four moons of Jupiter, the rings of Saturn including the black Cassini division in the rings, and stars in our neighbor Andromeda galaxy. The telescope was a resounding success. Poppa and Momma used to use the expression "When there's a will, there's a way." That proved true for me in making a telescope. Momma also used to say, "If wishes were horses, beggars could ride." I had learned that if you really wanted to do something, you had to do whatever work it required. That was a valuable lesson for a boy who often had big ideas at the beginning, and then sometimes failed to complete what he wished to do.

CHAPTER 48: *Upperclassman*

High School YPCA Executive Committee

$\mathcal{N}$ ow I was one of the older students. The younger students looked up to us. I served on the high school YPCA, Young People's Christian Association, executive committee. I played some basketball, but I often sat on the bench because there were many taller and better players than I was. I did well in track and field events in short sprints, high hurdles, high jump and even the pole vault. Some of my friends were already dating, but I felt rather shy with the girls and didn't date. There were strict rules about dating, and holding hands was not permitted. Some fellows and girls used short sticks to hold with their hands touching on the sticks so that technically they weren't holding hands. I was busy with my many activities outside of school, so I didn't have a lot of time to worry about such things as girls or dating.

The Junior Class students always presented a program for the Senior Class at what was called the Junior-Senior banquet. I must have left the impression with someone who planned the program that I was able to memorize and speak well in public because I was asked to tell a short story by memory at the banquet. I was quite nervous about this the evening of the banquet. The story was about a mean kid who was kidnapped by two naive guys who were trying to get paid a ransom. The mean kid knew how to make those two guys do all kinds of favors for him, so that they became the hostages instead, and ended up wanting to be able to get free of him.

We had our banquet meal first. I was having trouble eating, worrying about goofing up when I told the story. I had a tight feeling in the pit of my stomach when I was called to tell the story. As I was telling it, I had to be prompted several times, and that made me feel stupid. It was a funny story and the other students liked it, but I was sure glad when I was finished.

Our senior year of high school was 1958, which will go down in history as the year of the Sputnik. The Soviets had won this part of the race with their first satellite in space, and the United States was trying to learn all they could about it. Our astronomy teacher, Robert Lehman, formed us into a team to determine the orbit of Sputnik. As a senior, I was part of the Astral Society, which was an astronomy club made up mostly of college students. I volunteered to be one of the night watchers who would help pin down the satellite's orbit by determining its position in the sky.

Each observer sat at a small telescope that covered a certain portion of the sky. We sat in two lines at right angles to each other in such a way that one or more of us would surely see Sputnik in our scope. We were to observe the exact time that the satellite crossed our telescope's field of view. The satellite looked like a bright star or planet. But it was moving across the sky. We knew about where to look so we only needed to watch an hour or two in an evening. Someone would shout out when they first saw it with their naked eyes. Then we would all keep watching at our posts until it was gone from view. I did see Sputnik, but never got a location sighting through my spotting-scope.

My interest in astronomy continued for many years. March 7, 1970 was a special day for persons interested in astronomy. On that day there was to be a total eclipse of the sun along the east coast of United States. I had wanted to see a total solar eclipse, and this would be the best opportunity to do so, in years. Our oldest child, Tim, was four years old. I decided to take him with me, while my wife Susan took care of the rest of our family at home. We packed some lunches, a camera and some telescopic gear in our little VW bug. Tim was a good rider, and didn't seem to mind being off on an adventure with daddy.

We drove all the way to southeastern Virginia, across the state line a few miles into North Carolina, where we stopped the car out in the country. There were crows flying about and some chickens not too far away. It was getting to be the time for the eclipse as we munched some food. I projected the sun's image on a white sheet of paper on the ground. Pretty soon the black shadow of the moon was taking a bite out of the sun's disk. After while the sun became only a sliver of a crescent, but it still was daylight. I got my small telescope ready to take a picture.

Even though it was mid-day, it soon started to darken like the dusk of an evening. The crows cawed strangely, and a rooster crowed. The creatures around us seemed to be saying that night was coming. For an instant there was a bright bead of light on the edge of the moon, then it became dark. The bead of light was shining through a crater on the edge of the moon. The birds became quiet and went to roost. Now the sun's corona was just visible around the black disk of the moon which blotted out the rest of the sun. (See my picture.) In a few minutes it started to become light again. The crows started cawing. Again it was daylight, but the sun was only a crescent. We watched awhile longer, then headed for home.

We had to stop in Suffolk Virginia to fill the VW bug with gas, which I put on a charge card. We arrived home late from a memorable adventure, but one more unexpected thing happened. The credit card bill was over a hundred dollars for the nine or so gallons of gas that I had purchased. I called the credit card bank to explain the problem. They found that a dishonest gas attendant had added the cost of about 100 gallons of gas to what I had actually gotten. Thankfully, I did not have to pay the bill.

CHAPTER 49: *Graduation Time*

*G*raduation time in high school meant that the Senior Class would give a Class-day program for teachers, other students, friends and family. There would be a number of expected formalities such as singing a class song, the class President's address, presentation of a class gift to the school by our class treasurer, giving a "Key of Knowledge" to the Junior Class, and some special music. We had chosen "Christ Lead Onward" as our class motto. There was to be a competition for writing and composing the class song. I was not a musician, but I knew I could try my hand at some poetry or at least verse that might pass, so I submitted an entry. I did not win, but a team of fellow students came up with words and music for the song. The teachers who did the selection decided that my entry should be the class poem, and I was asked to recite it for our Class-day Program.

The day of the program came. My classmates all did a good job with their parts. I felt that I was better prepared than I had been at the Junior Senior Program. I had worked so hard in writing the poem that I almost knew it without memorizing. I did get through my Poet Lauriat presentation without goofing up as I had with the short story for the previous year's seniors. I was thankful. This is the poem:

"Christ Lead Onward.

When as eager youth, O Lord, we mount the upward way,

To meet each challenge and gain new heights to follow thee, We pray, give us new vigor when we may weary be,

To bravely thus declare; Our saving Christ lead onward.

Lord to Thee we give our lives to climb this rugged path,

And to help the wayward find this way that leads to Thee.

Give faith to follow on though the path we cannot see,

And grant us faith to say; Our guiding Christ, lead onward.

Let us ever onward press and gain the greater height,

Until the top is won and to Christ our praise we give.

Oh, Christ, help us to see this goal and for Thee to live.

We'll ever sing to Thee; Our loving Christ lead onward."

This is certainly not a song, but it did express the sentiments that I was feeling as a senior ready to graduate and move beyond high school. Being able to give it was an affirmation that I needed and am thankful for, even today.

CHAPTER 50: *A Glimpse of the Future*

$\mathcal{I}$ attended college at Eastern Mennonite so it was not so great a shift in my experience, since I did not have to move away from home. I majored in chemistry, but took lots of math courses. As a senior I realized that I had taken enough math courses for a major. I went to the Registrar's Office and told them that I also had a math major and was accepted. I had several opportunities to teach before I graduated. Once the math professor was ill and asked me to teach his college algebra class for a class period that he would need to miss. So as a college junior, I taught a college class for one day. Then as a senior, there was a shortage of staff in the chemistry department, so I became an organic chemistry lab instructor in my senior year.

I still hadn't dated much, partly because I also was working night shift as a hospital orderly. In my sophomore year at college, there was a class party where the girls all ask the fellows for dates. I was asked and accepted. That was my first college date. After college I was invited to stay on as a faculty assistant in the chemistry department. I had applied and been accepted at Virginia Tech for a research assistantship. I studied there in the summer, and then returned to Eastern Mennonite College to teach beginning chemistry classes, quantitative analysis and organic chemistry labs.

Dr. D. Ralph Hostetter, who was a biologist, became my mentor. One of the classes I taught was an all-female class consisting of nursing and home economics majors. They didn't like the tests I made up very well, so they decided to all come to class for an exam dressed in black!, I failed to notice what they did, until someone told me! On the last day of my teaching that class, the students all came dressed in white, and I did notice that! Some of my students were older than I was.

I had started dating by now. I met Susan Hershey Leaman, who came to college as a registered nurse to get a B.S.N. degree. We got married the summer after her graduation, in 1964. We were blessed with three children, Timothy, Aletha, and Theodore in a little less than four years. This made for an active household. We often drove into the mountains to get out into nature, which we all enjoyed. We had a number of little adventures that led to a whole menagerie of pets.

Once we caught a small green snake and took it home and put it into an empty glass aquarium that had a lid. The children named the snake Emerald. The children also found several other small snakes around our house. You can see a picture of our three children each holding a small snake.

Our favorite wild pet was Peter the chipmunk. He was half-grown when we got him. Instead of dashing into a hole when we came by, he had scampered up a small oak tree, but was almost frozen by fright. I reached up and caught him. I made a cage for him, and a wheel that he could run in, just like the larger one that Mr. Mumaw had made for the foxes. We fed Peter mostly grains.

He was a very neat housekeeper. He chewed paper into small pieces to make his sleeping nest. Another corner of the cage was the bathroom. He loved to run in his exercise wheel and to eat in his dining area. He became quite tame. Unfortunately, he came to a sad end. Our son Theo had a big gray, tiger striped cat that we called Bobcat. Most of the time Bobcat lived outside, but we often let him into the house. One time, we left the house in a hurry, with Bobcat still in the house. When we got home, Peter's cage was knocked on the floor, with the top open. Bobcat was not too far away with, shall I say, a contented, well-fed look. We never found a single hair of Peter or any other evidence of what might have happened, but we were pretty sure that Peter couldn't have escaped the house.

The things that I loved doing growing up spilled over into my family. Now our three grandchildren, Audrey, Luc, and Ben have some of the same interests.

In later years, I became a Sunday school teacher to the man who had been Poppa's boss in the hatchery box room. He still called me Johnny while everyone else called me John.

In "The Manger Is Empty" Walter Wangerin, Jr. tells of a boyhood experience of touching a cicada wing shortly after it emerged from its underground nymph shell. That wing did not form right, but oozed a dazzling emerald drop of its lifeblood. "And this is what I say today, When cicadas tear the air with their incessant sawing, that is God making furniture. He's cutting wood for a cradle and a cross. And Christ on the cross is more beautiful than anything – for extreme pain is the cost of extremist beauty." His pain turns the scars of our metamorphosis into beauty.

Johnny has met John.

Jimmy king of the roof. Solar eclipse.

John and young son Tim traveled to North Carolina to get this picture of a total eclipse of the sun on March 7, 1970.

Eyepiece
Eyepiece Mount
Light
Diagonal

Light

Mirror

The viewer looks into the eyepiece but sees what is reflected by the mirror.

John's Reflector Telescope Design

Telescope plan and Sputnik Moonwatch Team.